how to
ENTERTAIN
CHILDREN
with magic
YOU
can do

by The Great Merlini

A Fireside Book
Published by Simon and Schuster

A Fireside Book
Published by Simon and Schuster
Rockefeller Center, 630 Fifth Avenue
New York, New York 10020

First Fireside paperback printing 1971
SBN 671-21056-4 Fireside paperback edition
Library of Congress Catalog Card Number: 62-14283
Designed by Betty Crumley
Manufactured in the United States of America

For my favorite magician's assistants
BUTCH, SALLY, JO *and* HUGH

PREFACE

CLAYTON RAWSON, *using his alias, The Great Merlini, has here put together a book of magic that really is easy to perform — and fun to do. His long experience as a writer and editor has enabled him to explain the tricks in clear, nontechnical language. He also stresses something too often overlooked — that the best magic should be entertaining as well as mystifying, and that this depends upon dramatic presentation. He takes pains to explain in detail how the beginner can achieve this at the start.* How to Entertain Children with Magic YOU Can Do *is an excellent introduction to magic, not only for the adult who wants to entertain children but for the young beginner as well.*

JOHN SCARNE

CONTENTS

3 : SORCERY WITH STRING

4 : ROPE AND KNOT MAGIC

5 : TRICKS WITH EVERYTHING

6 : SELF-WORKING CARD TRICKS

7 : EASY SLEIGHT OF HAND WITH CARDS

8 : PREPARED CARD MIRACLES

9 : HOW TO READ MINDS

10 : MAGICAL PARTY STUNTS

INTRODUCTION

A fairy tale on the printed page excites a child's wonder and stretches his imagination. Drama is added when it is read or told by a good storyteller. Magic adds an extra dimension. A magic trick, well presented, is a fairy tale come alive. The magician is himself a storyteller and the wonders he relates appear to happen. This is why all children are fascinated by magic.

If you can do even one trick that is really magical you can command any child's instant attention. If you can do several, you are Superman, Merlin, and a fairy godmother all in one. It is a sure-fire way to make friends of, and influence, children.

A question which all magicians hear constantly from parents, grandparents, and teachers, from leaders of Cub Scouts, Boy Scouts, Girl Scouts, and Campfire Girls, from anyone who has or who works with children is this, "Are there a few simple tricks I could learn to do for my kids?" And they usually add, "Of course, my fingers are all thumbs and I couldn't learn any sleight of hand."

We have good news. Magic consists in doing or appearing to do the impossible. This sounds difficult and magicians are careful not to contradict this notion. On the contrary, because it is good showmanship, they pretend that all tricks, even easy ones, require great skill. But all magic is not as difficult as it may look. Sometimes the most difficult-appearing tricks are actually accomplished by very simple means. And often a trick which the spectators believe must require difficult sleight of hand uses some quite different method and may require little or no manual dexterity at all.

We have more good news. The phrase *sleight of hand* implies manual dexterity, but sleight of hand does not always require a special talent and long hours of practice. Some of it can be done by anyone who can accomplish such simple actions as tying a knot or shuffling a deck of cards.

Magicians have long pretended that the hand is quicker than the eye. This is another red herring to mislead audiences. The hand is not quicker than the eye; it does not need to be. The real secret is more subtle. The important principles of deception are more psychological than visual. The magician is more concerned with misdirecting the mind than fooling the eye. He induces his audience to make false assumptions, think illogically, and draw wrong conclusions, so that they end by believing that something happened which did not happen. And you do not need to have a degree as a psychologist to accomplish this. Some tricks are so designed that the psychological misdirection is built in and works automatically. These are the tricks you will find here.

Some of the tricks that follow are so nearly automatic that you will be able to do them as soon as you have read the instructions. These have been placed at the beginning of each chapter and, if you have not previously done any magic, these are the tricks you should learn first. Concentrate on one or two at a time; don't complicate things by trying to learn too many all at once. Begin by learning a few, and then expand your repertoire gradually.

Remember that reading the instructions and learning the secret of a trick does not make you a magician. Magic is a performing art and is best learned by doing. But don't step out in front of a dozen or more children and attempt for the first time a trick you have just learned. Use your family as a rehearsal audience; try it on them first. This will give you the confidence you will need to perform before other and larger audiences. Confidence is all important. A magician who is unsure of himself is a contradiction in terms, and his pretense of having magic powers is less than convincing.

Since there is no real magic, a magician is an actor pretending to be a magician. And, like any actor, he acquires the confidence and facility he needs through practice and rehearsal. You won't need to spend long hours in acquiring digital dexterity to perform the tricks you find here, but you should rehearse them enough so that you can present them smoothly and without a hitch.

Since the magician is an actor, a magic trick is a short dramatic sketch, and the instructions for doing a trick are his acting script. At least they should be. Trick instructions for the beginner are often so abbreviated that only part of the script is given. The mechanics of the trick, the secret of *what* makes it work are explained, but little or nothing is said about a much more important matter: *how* the trick should be performed.

An old and very true maxim among professional magicians is, "It is not so much what you do as how you do it." A beginner who has learned a trick from instructions that neglect to tell him how to present it may manage to fool his audience, but the trick is never as effective nor as entertaining as it could be. He discovers this when he sees a professional perform the same trick and get far more applause. The difference is that the beginner has gone through all the motions and only managed to present the bare bones of the trick. He has simply propounded a puzzle which could, properly presented, have been transformed into a feat that seems really magical and far more interesting to watch.

We have tried here to supply complete acting scripts which give not only the mechanics but also the dramatic presentations that add the interest and suspense and humor which will make your magic entertaining.

Learn the mechanics first. Study the instructions with the necessary props in hand. This is especially important with card tricks. If you have the cards in hand and perform each action as you read, directions which at first glance may seem complicated become not only much easier to follow but are much more quickly memorized.

After you have learned the physical action, study the presentation. Learn your lines. These are set in italic both to emphasize their importance and as an aid to study. Don't try to improvise your lines as you perform. They are too important. They are what make the trick entertaining, and it is also in what you say and how you say it that much of the misdirection lies on which your deception depends. Later, when you have had more experience, you may want to fit different words to the music, but at the beginning stick to the script; it's safer.

You can be fully confident of one thing at the start. When you perform for children you have a willing and eager audience. You should be warned that kids en masse are sometimes too helpful. Don't ever ask for a volunteer when you need an assistant. They are all so eager to get into the act that you may be trampled by the thundering herd. Go into the audience, pick out the child you want, and bring him back.

Even this sometimes creates an uproar as they all shout offers of assistance. Counter this with, "I never use noisy assistants; only quiet ones." This usually restores some measure of order to the proceedings.

You should, perhaps, be warned about Cub Scouts. They are the world's noisiest audience. They whistle loudly and continuously. Don't try to raise your voice above this pandemonium; it isn't possible. Stop, put your hands over your ears, and wait. Eventually they get the idea that the show isn't going to proceed under these conditions and the hullabaloo dies down. An announcement at this point that you will award a special merit badge to the quietest Scout often helps. Then, once or twice after a trick, make good on this offer and pay off with a nickel or dime.

Both the kind of tricks that you do and the length of your program should be determined by the age level of your audience. If most of the group are too young to be able to tell one card from another omit the card tricks. For small children three or four tricks at one time may be sufficient. As they get older and their attention span lengthens you can do more. But don't stay on too long; always stop while they are still asking for more. Formal programs for groups of some size can run longer, but it is always best to stop too soon rather than too late.

Make sure that you have rehearsed each trick you do sufficiently, so that it goes off smoothly and without a hitch. This is even more important when performing for children than adults, because a child who sees something you didn't intend him to see can't resist saying so promptly in a loud voice. This draws everyone's attention to the mistake. Adults, more inhibited, are much less likely to do this. They are also aware that your magic powers are pretended and that you are acting a part, and they don't feel that they must try to expose you. Children, more literal minded, take your claim to be a wonder-worker at face value and are disillusioned if they see anything that contradicts this. They are also disappointed. They prefer to believe in Santa Claus; they want the magic to be real. Don't let them down.

If you like kids you will have a lot of fun doing the magic in this book. No matter how much time and effort you put into it you will be repaid many times over by the wide-eyed enchantment on their faces and the excited wonder in their eyes as the magic happens.

how to
ENTERTAIN
CHILDREN
with magic
YOU
can do

MATCH MAGIC

matchless mind reading

The performer reads the minds of the spectators and discovers which one of several match folders was selected behind his back.

Collect several match folders bearing different designs and place them on a table.

"I have discovered something," you say, "which will put the telephone company out of business. I have found out how to know what people are thinking before they tell me. Let's try it. When my back is turned I want someone to select one of these match folders, open it, tear out a match, close the folder, and put it back with the others."

Turn your back until this is done.

"Now, I am going to hold each folder to my forehead and

concentrate. When I am holding the selected folder I want you all to think, 'That's it!' just as hard as you can."

You do this and find the selected folder. The method is extremely simple. At the beginning, as you collect and set out the folders, you push the flap of each folder down tightly behind the sandpaper strip. When the spectator opens a folder, tears out a match, and recloses the folder, he never pushes the flap in firmly. This is your clue. When you pick up each folder, hold it between thumb and forefinger, the thumb on the flap. Push the flap toward the sandpaper strip. The folder whose flap moves slightly is the one that was selected.

The trick seems even more like real mind reading if you keep your eyes closed throughout, or, better still, do it blindfolded.

upside-down matches

A box of safety matches is turned upside down and the drawer is removed. The matches defy gravity: they do not fall out until commanded to do so.

You prepare for this one in advance by breaking a match in two and wedging it crosswise in the drawer (fig. 1). Then proceed as follows:

Display the matchbox and push the drawer out a little less than halfway so the spectators can see that it contains matches. Remove one match, close the drawer, and turn the box upside down.

"Did you know that if you hold a matchbox upside down and then pass one match around it three times in a clockwise direction this repeals the law of gravity so that the matches won't fall out when the drawer is removed?"

Push the upside-down drawer out, then hold it at the ends between thumb and forefinger (fig 1).

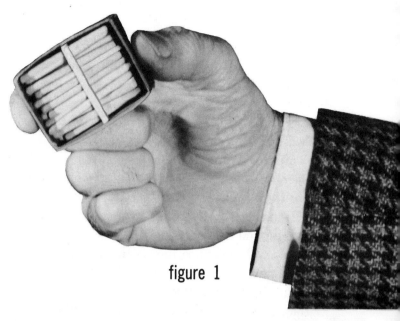

figure 1

"And if you make the same mystic pass around the box in the other direction, it breaks the spell."

You do this and the matches promptly fall from the drawer — because you squeeze the ends of the drawer slightly. This bends the sides of the drawer and releases the half-match, which then falls with, and is hidden by, the others.

Now use the matches for the **Scrambled Arithmetic** trick which follows.

scrambled arithmetic

A curiously baffling problem in arithmetic which becomes more baffling with each repetition.

"When you do arithmetic you are given a problem and you have to figure out the answer. Let me show you how to get a correct answer without even knowing what the problem is. Here are some matches. While my back is turned, make three piles of matches. Put the same number in each pile, but make it hard for me by putting at least four matches in each pile.

"You are going to add and subtract some matches, and when you finish I'll tell you how many matches are in the center pile even though I don't know how many matches there are at the beginning."

Step 1.   *"Take three matches from each of the end piles and put them in the center pile."*

Step 2.   *"Count the matches that remain in either one of the end piles, take that many away from the center pile, and put them in the left-hand pile."*

It makes no difference how many matches are being used; at this point the center pile will always contain *nine* matches. You could announce this as the answer, but don't. Ask the spectator to transfer a few more matches from pile to pile, mentally keeping track of what these additions and subtractions do to the nine in the center pile.

For example, have five matches transferred from the left pile to the center pile (9 plus 5 is 14), then have three matches moved from the center pile to either end pile (14 minus 3 is 11). Give this as the answer. Since you know that the center pile contains nine matches after Step 2, you can bring the final total to whatever you like.

The spectators may suspect that you are using some system which always produces the same answer. Disprove this by repeating the stunt and getting a different final total. Point out also that the spectator can begin each time with a different number of matches. The only restrictions are that the three piles must be equal at the beginning and that each must contain four or more matches.

You can confuse the issue even more by varying the procedure in Step 1. Instead of asking to have three matches transferred, have only one or two moved. If one match is transferred, the number of matches in the center pile, after Step 2, will be three. If two matches are moved, the center pile will contain six; if three are moved, it will contain nine. The center pile, after Step 2, *always* contains three times the number you use in Step 1.

Since you can arrive at any total you like, you can also predict the answer even before the spectator decides how many matches he will use.

When asked how it is done, say, *"Nobody knows, but you don't need to know. Oddly enough, anybody can do it. You name any number between 1 and 12, the first one that comes into your mind."*

Repeat the trick, bringing the final total to the spectator's number.

"The answer is always whatever you want it to be. Wouldn't it be nice if they taught this kind of arithmetic in school?"

The fact that you never give the same instructions twice, since you don't know how many matches are being used, makes this trick a real mystery.

the tramps and the geese

This one is for the small fry. Older children may sometimes figure it out, but the smaller ones like it for the story.

Hold one match in each hand and put five on the table. *"The five matches are five geese and the two I hold are hungry tramps walking along the road on Thanksgiving Day with nothing to eat. They see the geese and one tramp says, 'Look, Joe, there's our dinner.' Joe says, 'Oh, boy!' and he grabs one goose and puts it under his coat."*

As you say this, pick up one of the geese with the *right* hand and hold it in your fist together with the match representing the first tramp.

"Then Sam took a goose, too. Then they took all the geese." Pick up the rest of the matches one at a time with alternate hands.

"Just then they heard the farmer coming and Sam said, 'Maybe we'd better put the geese back.' So they did."

Lay the matches down, one at a time, from alternate hands, but start with the *left* hand. When the five geese have been replaced, you'll find that you have no matches in your left fist, two in your right.

"*The farmer didn't stay long, and as soon as he had gone the two hungry tramps picked up the geese again.*" Do as before but start picking up with the *right* hand.

"*Then Joe, the thin tramp, said, 'Sam, I know why you are fatter than I am. Somehow you always get more geese.'*"

Open both fists and show two matches in the left hand and five in the right.

"*This made Sam so mad he got into a fight with Joe. Meanwhile, all the geese ran home, had a Thanksgiving dinner of their own, and lived happily ever after.*"

the illusive spots

The most effective and most intriguing of all tricks are those in which the magic happens visibly. In this one a penciled spot appears mysteriously on a paper match. It jumps suddenly to a second match, then back again to the first one. A second spot appears on the reverse side of the match, then both spots jump across to the second match and back again. Both matches then acquire spots on both sides and finally, all four spots vanish. This is the best of all match tricks; it looks like real magic.

In advance, secretly prepare two paper matches by drawing a spot or cross mark with pencil or pen on each match on one side only at the end opposite the head. If you mark all the matches in the front row of a folder in this way, you are always ready to do the trick simply by tearing out two matches.

You need to be able to do one very simple sleight-of-hand move, which can be learned in a moment or two. Hold one of the prepared matches with its head between your thumb and forefinger, the blank side showing (fig. 2A). Push the thumb toward the end of the forefinger, causing the match to make a half-turn. This simple half-twist of the match is the move that does the whole trick, but the spectators never see it. Here's why.

Display the match as in fig. 2A, then turn the hand over to the left so that it is palm down (fig. 2B). Twist the match while the hand is turning. The small half-twist of the match passes unseen because the hand is in motion. Don't turn the hand too fast; quick motions arouse suspicion. Turn it just as you would if you were showing both sides of the match naturally. You will find that you can turn your hand quite slowly without the secret twist being seen.

Now turn the hand palm up, again. As you do so, pull the thumb inward, giving the match a twist in the opposite direction. You will appear to have shown both sides of the match quite fairly, although actually the same side has been shown twice.

Now, instead of turning the hand over, simply move it quickly a few inches to the right, then back again. Make the secret twist at the same time. This causes the previously unseen spot to appear suddenly.

Again turn the hand over and back, but this time, do not make the secret move. Simply show the match top and bottom without sleight of hand. One side has a spot, the other is blank.

Turn the hand once more, and make the secret move. Both sides of the match will now seem to have spots.

This secret action of giving the match a half-twist, which is sometimes hidden by turning the hand over and sometimes by giving a quick shake, sets you up in business as a sleight-of-hand artist. Now run through the procedure given below a few times. It is an easy routine to memorize because each action logically follows the preceding one. When you have

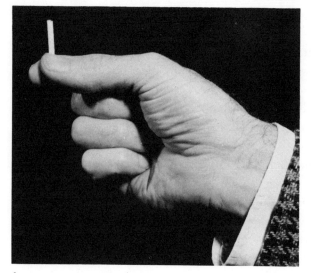

A

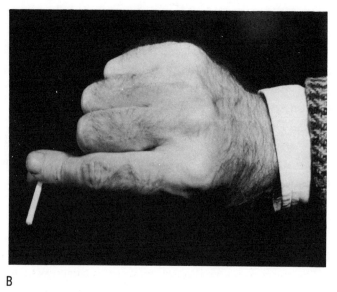

B

figure 2

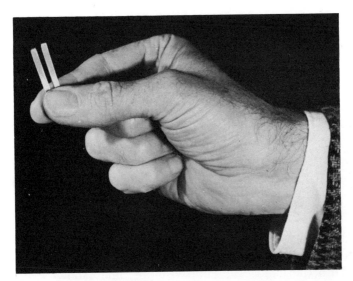

C

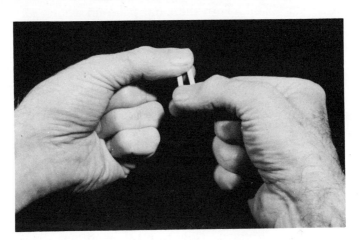

E D

learned it, you will find yourself doing a magic routine in which there are several magical surprises and a mystifying climax.

1. Hold *two* matches, each of which has a spot on its underside, as shown in fig. 2C. Turn the hand over, making the secret move, apparently showing that the other sides are also blank. Turn the hand back again (making the move). (You will find that the secret move can be made just as easily with two matches as with one.)

2. Take away the left-hand match with the left hand. Shake the right hand (making the move), causing the spot to appear.

3. Turn the hand over (no twist this time) showing the other side blank. Turn the hand palm up again.

4. Put the second match back in the right hand. Shake the hand (making the move), and the spot appears to jump from match to match.

5. Shake the hand again (making the move), and the spot jumps back to its original position.

6. Remove the blank match from the right hand. Turn the right hand over and show that a second spot has appeared. This match now has spots on both sides. Turn the hand back. (Make the secret move both times.)

7. Put the second match back in the right hand. Shake the hand (making the move). The visible spot again jumps from match to match. Now turn the hand over (making the move) and show that the spot on the other side of the match has also jumped across. Turn the hand palm up again (making the move).

8. Take the spotted match in the left hand. Shake the blank match (making the move), and a third spot appears. Show that the underside is still blank (turning the hand without the move).

9. Blow on the match. Turn the hand again (with the move), and a fourth spot is seen.

10. Hold both matches in the right hand. Turn the hand (making the move), and you are showing four spots, one on each side of each match.

Now say, *"You may think you are wide awake. Actually you are daydreaming. None of this has really happened."*

11. Shake the right hand (making the move), and both spots vanish. Then turn the hand over (making the move), and there are no spots on that side either.

Finally, toss the matches to the spectator. He examines them and finds that there really are no spots anywhere!

What he gets are two unmarked matches. You have been holding these concealed under the curled second, third, and fourth fingers of your left hand from the beginning of the trick.

The switch is made very simply. Bring the left hand over to the visible matches and take them between thumb and forefinger as in fig. 2D. Your left hand seems to toss these two matches to the spectator. Actually, you simply turn your left hand palm down and open your curled fingers (fig. 2E). The opening fingers release the hidden, unprepared matches and cover the others. While the spectator is examining the matches, drop those you still hold into your pocket. If you are seated at a table, simply bring the left hand to the table's edge and let the matches fall into your lap.

You'll have fun with this trick. The effect on the spectator will more than repay you for the small amount of practice which is necessary.

A word about paper matches. Some are white or yellow on one side, gray on the other. Avoid these. Use matches that are the same color on both sides.

Even better, using a razor blade, cut two pieces of wood from a tongue depressor. Make them the same width as a paper match, but half again as long. Use black ink for the spots. The trick is such a good one that it is well worth this extra trouble.

CONJURING WITH COINS

the invisible coin

A coin becomes invisible. When pushed into one ear it reappears in the other, visible again.

Hold any small coin on the right fingertips. Bend your left arm, putting the hand near the left ear. Place the coin on the left elbow, cover it with the right fingers, and rub it with a circular motion.

"Did you know that if you rub a coin against your elbow like this, it becomes smaller and smaller?" As you say this, lift your fingers slightly and allow the coin to drop to the floor as though accidentally.

"It'll never work if I do that." Bend down and pick up the coin with the fingers of the *left* hand. Pretend to transfer the coin from the left to the right hand, but actually retain it in

the left fingers. You simply place the left fingers on the right palm, close the right hand, and return immediately to your original position, left hand near the ear, right hand on the elbow. Don't feel guilty about this action and don't do it too fast; that will only create suspicion. Just do it naturally.

Continue rubbing the right fingers against the elbow. Meanwhile, the left fingers secretly push the coin into your left ear. *"This rubbing gradually wears the coin away until it becomes very thin."*

Pretend to take the now invisible coin from the elbow and place it on the left palm. *"This is probably the thinnest coin you ever saw!"* Both hands at this point are seen to be empty.

Pick up the phantom coin. *"With a really thin coin like this I can do a remarkable thing. If I push it into my right ear like this, it passes right through my head — there isn't anything much there to stop it — and comes out of my left ear."*

Reach into your left ear and bring out the coin which has become visible again.

A variation: Instead of leaving the coin in your ear, push it into your collar, thus accomplishing a complete vanish. Finish by showing that the coin has been rubbed into invisibility and then give it to someone as a souvenir. *"Don't try to spend it for candy. They'll give you invisible candy, and that — you can't even taste."*

the vanishing coin

A coin vanish that can be used in several ways.

Place a penny on the back of the left fist. Cover it with the right fingers, begin to rub it against the fist, and then, accidentally let it fall to the floor. As you go to get it, put your left foot beside it. Bend down and pick up the coin with your right hand. As you straighten up, let your hand pass close to your right ankle, and allow the coin to slide off the fingers into your trouser cuff. Don't push it in; just drop it without pausing as your hand goes past. The spectators won't see this. If an action seems important they watch it carefully. But here they believe the coin was dropped accidentally, so they pay little attention to the way it is picked up.

Place the fingers on the back of the fist again and continue rubbing. *"If I do this just right, the coin will pass through my hand."* After a moment lift the fingers slowly, showing that the coin has gone. Then turn the left hand over, open it, and find nothing. *"I must have rubbed it a little too hard. I lose a lot of money that way."*

A variation: Hold a quarter concealed in your left hand at the start. And finish by saying, *"The nice thing about this trick is that when the penny goes through the hand it becomes larger. Twenty-five times larger. I make a lot of money this way."*

penny-to-dime

A penny placed in a spectator's hand changes to a dime.

Take several coins from your pocket and place them on your left palm. Pick up a dime, slide it with the thumb to the base of the right third and fourth fingers and close them over it. (This method of holding a coin concealed in the hand is called the *finger palm* and is shown in fig. 3A.) Now pick up one or two more coins in the usual manner, say, *"We won't need these,"* and put them back in your pocket. But retain the dime in the finger palm.

Remaining in your left hand you should have a penny, either a quarter or a fifty-cent piece, and one or two other coins. Arrange these on the hand so that they can all be seen, but see that the largest coin is behind and slightly overlaps the penny (fig. 3B). Name each coin and ask a spectator to add them. *"I have fifty cents, a penny, and two nickels. How much is that altogether?"*

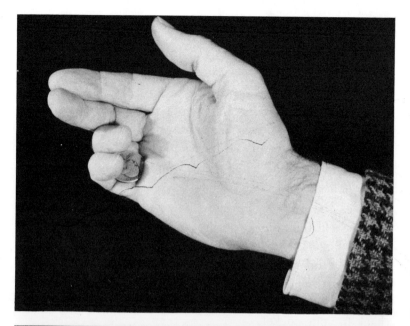

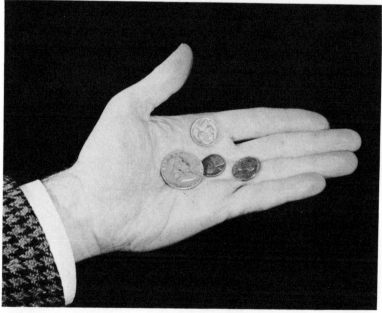

figure 3

When the spectator gives the answer, ask, *"And if I take away a penny, what does that leave?"*

As you say this you apparently pick up the penny with the thumb and first two fingers of your right hand. When your hand is above the penny, momentarily hiding it, your fingers push it back under the larger coin.

The child replies, "Sixty cents," and you say, *"Very good. Now hold out your hand."*

Place the tips of your right fingers (which the spectator thinks hold the penny) on his hand and open the third and fourth fingers, allowing the concealed dime to fall onto his palm. At the same time say, *"Now close your hand tightly."* Take your hand away just as he does this. He will feel the dime but think that he has the penny. Put all the other coins back in your pocket.

"Hold the penny tightly. I'm going to try to make it disappear at the count of three. Are you ready? It's still there? Good. One. Two. Three. Go! Do you still feel it? You do? Are you sure? That's funny. This has always worked before. Let me see it." He opens his hand and finds that the penny has changed to a dime.

There is one drawback to this trick — the child always wants you to do it again. It's usually not wise to repeat the same trick immediately. So you proceed to do the trick that follows, making the dime disappear.

into thin air

A coin vanishes into thin air — then mysteriously reappears.

Display a coin on the left palm. Pick it up with the right hand and hold it about a foot above the left hand. *"Watch what happens when I say 'Go!'"*

Bring the coin down, touch the left palm with it, and

count, *"One."* Raise the coin again, higher this time, bring it back to the palm, counting, *"Two."* Lift it once more, place it, without hesitating, on the top of your head and leave it there. Immediately bring the now empty hand down to the left palm, close the left fingers, and count, *"Three."* As you remove your right hand, turn it palm up so that it is seen to be empty.

Snap your fingers and say, *"Go!"* Then frown and add, *"No, it's still there. I'll try again."* Snap your fingers twice. *"Go! That's better."* Open the hand slowly showing that the coin has vanished.

Then say, *"I wonder if we can make it reappear?"* Ask the child to hold his hands in front of him, side by side, pronounce any magic spell you like, and tilt your head. The missing coin drops from nowhere into the child's hands.

the penetrating coin

A half dollar visibly penetrates a borrowed handkerchief.

Hold a half dollar upright between the finger tips and thumb of the left hand. You may use your own handkerchief but the trick is more effective if you use one belonging to a spectator. Lay the handkerchief over the left hand, adjusting it so that the coin is at its center. Then grasp the coin through the handkerchief momentarily between the right thumb and forefinger. Push the left thumb upward slightly making a small fold in the cloth behind the coin at its base (fig. 4A).

Let someone feel the coin through the cloth. Then, to further convince him everything is honest, grasp the front edge of the handkerchief with the right hand and lift it up and back onto the arm. Lower the left hand at the same time so that the coin points downward. This partially exposes the coin so that everyone can see that it is still there (fig. 4B).

The right fingers, which still hold the front edge of the

handkerchief, now also grasp the rear edge which is lying on the arm, and then carry both edges forward and down, covering the coin. The coin appears to be fairly covered, but it is actually behind and outside of the handkerchief.

Grasp the handkerchief a few inches below the coin and twist it, drawing the cloth tightly around the coin. Grip the handkerchief with the second, third, and fourth fingers of the right hand, and press the thumb and forefinger against opposite edges of the coin (fig. 4C).

"Most magic takes place under cover, where you can't see it. This time it happens in full view. Watch! When I squeeze the coin, it passes right through the center of the handkerchief!"

Keep your left forefinger under the coin but lift your left thumb. Squeeze the edges of the coin with the right fingers, slowly pushing it into view. The illusion that it is being pushed right through the cloth is perfect.

"Of course," you add, *"that ruins the handkerchief, but if I blow on it gently, the hole mends itself."* Toss the handkerchief to its owner so that he can see for himself.

coin through table

Solid passes through solid again. A surprising, quick trick to be done at the dinner table.

You have two half dollars in your pocket. Both hands go below the edge of the table and the right hand goes into the pocket for the coins. As the right hand comes out; secretly drop one coin into the left hand and bring the other up into view. Lean forward, give the coin to someone, and ask that it be examined to make sure that it is genuine and quite solid. As he is doing this, extend your left hand under the table, place the second coin on your knee, and leave it there.

Take the first coin back from the spectator and place it on

A

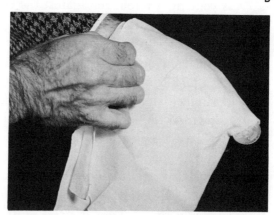

B

figure 4

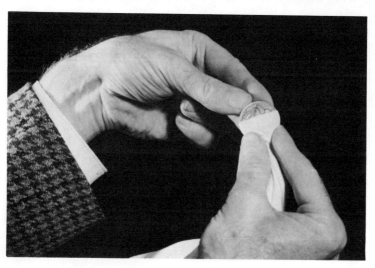

C

the table directly in front of you, five or six inches from the edge of the table. Show both hands, front and back, so that it is obvious that they are empty. Say, *"Watch!"* Cover the coin with the right fingers, pull it back to the table edge, pick it up, move the hand forward, and slap it down on the table. Press down on it and rub it against the table with a circular motion.

While this is going on, put your left hand under the table, pick up the coin from the knee, and hold it on the fingers, the hand palm up. Say, *"This doesn't seem to be working."* Lift the right hand and show the coin, then slide it back and leave it five or six inches from the table edge as before.

Press your right forefinger against the center of the table-top in two or three places as you say, *"I'm sure there's a soft spot here somewhere. Oh yes, here it is."*

Cover the coin again, slide it to the edge of the table, and pretend to pick it up, but this time let it drop into your lap instead. Immediately move your right hand forward and slap it down on the table as before; at the same time, your left hand slaps the coin it holds up against the underside of the table. The sound of the coin hitting the table seems to indicate that it is still under the right hand.

Go through the pressing and rubbing motions as before, then suddenly say, *"There it goes!"* Lift your right hand, showing that the coin has gone. Pause a moment, then bring the left hand up and drop the coin on the table.

the evaporating coin

The magician announces a very special trick, one that is seldom seen because it is so difficult. He shows a half dollar and states that he intends to make it disappear under the strictest possible test conditions. He gives the coin to someone to examine while he removes his coat and rolls up his left shirt sleeve. He asks the spectator to testify that the coin is a regulation and quite solid fifty-cent piece, then holds out his hand and asks that it be placed in the center of his palm.

Then he spreads out a handkerchief (preferably borrowed) and lays it carefully over the coin and the hand. All this is done slowly so that the audience will be quite satisfied that no sleight of hand is possible. To emphasize this further he asks a spectator to reach in under the handkerchief and feel the coin to be sure that it is still there. Two or three other spectators are asked to do the same.

Then, still in slow motion and without any sign of a suspicious move, he says dramatically, "*Watch! One, two, three — go!*" He pulls the handkerchief away slowly. His hand is empty; the coin has gone. The handkerchief is tossed to the audience. "*I'm not sure*," the performer says, "*how that's done myself.*"

Does it sound difficult? It's supposed to. That's part of the misdirection. It's actually very easy. This trick illustrates perfectly that in magic it is not so much what you do as how you do it. The half dollar vanishes into thin air because the last spectator to reach under the handkerchief to assure himself that the coin was there is your confederate. He simply takes it away.

It is the selling job you do that is important. If you are dead serious about everything you say and do and convince the audience that they are about to witness a miracle — that's what they'll see.

multiplying money

The magician gives a spectator a pencil to use as a magic wand and shows several coins whose total is added. When the child waves his wand over the coins and then recounts them, he finds that the total has increased. This is repeated twice more.

Conceal a fifty-cent piece in your right hand before the trick begins. Ask a child if he would like to do some magic. Reach under your coat, drop the half dollar into the armhole of your left sleeve, and bring a pencil from your pocket. Raise the left arm a bit so that when the half dollar slides down the sleeve it will stop at the elbow.

Give the pencil to the spectator, then reach into your right pocket and bring out several coins. Hold them on the palm of your right hand a bit above the spectator's eye level. Spread the coins with your left fingers as though counting them and place a quarter on the third joint of the third finger (fig. 5A).

Close the fingers half-way, and dump the coins into the left hand. The curled third finger prevents the quarter from falling with the other coins (fig. 5A).

Spread the coins on the left palm, and again push one coin — a nickel perhaps — on to the third joint of the third finger (fig. 5B). Show the coins and ask the spectator how much money you have. When he announces the total, dump the coins back into the right hand and close it. This time retain the nickel in the left hand.

Tell the child to wave his wand three times over your closed hand. Then open it and have him recount the coins. The total has increased by twenty cents.

"You did that very well. Would you like to try it again?" The answer is always, "Yes."

Dump the coins back into the left hand again. The wand is waved again and this time the total increases by five cents.

Transfer the coins to the right hand and have the wand waved again. As this is being done, drop your left hand to your side and let the half dollar in your sleeve slide down and fall into your curled fingers.

Open the right hand. This time the value of the coins has not increased. *"Well,"* you say, *"I sometimes have that trouble, too. I don't think you waved the wand hard enough. Try it again."* Dump the coins back into the left hand. The wand is waved — harder this time — and the total jumps by fifty cents!

"That's the way to do it! You've made so much money for me that you deserve a commission." Give the child a coin to keep.

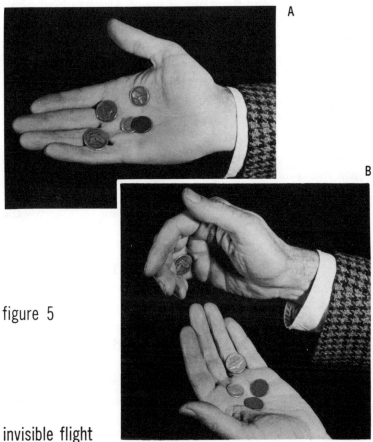

A

B

figure 5

invisible flight

A borrowed and marked half dollar is held in the performer's fist. His hand is covered with a handkerchief which is fastened around the wrist with a rubber band so that coin and hand are completely enclosed. In spite of all these precautions, the coin leaves the hand and travels invisibly through the air, and reappears in a hat on the other side of the room.

Borrow a hat (or use your own), and ask a spectator to make sure there is nothing in it. Then place it on the opposite side of the room.

Borrow a half dollar. If none of the small fry present are that well-to-do, lend them one of yours. Also hand out a soft pencil and ask that the coin be marked.

While the marking is being done, obtain another fifty-cent piece from your pocket and hold it finger-palmed in your right hand (fig. 3A). Take the marked coin in your left hand, close it, and say, *"This marked coin is going to leave my hand and fly across the room into the empty hat. Would you like to see it go visibly or invisibly?"*

They almost always want to see it go visibly, which is the reply you want. But if not, you say, *"Let's do it both ways. When it goes visibly, it looks like this."* Simply open your hand, pick up the coin with the right hand, walk across the room to the hat, and place the coin in it. Secretly leave the second coin there at the same time.

"That really isn't much of a trick, is it? Let's do it the hard way — invisibly." Reach into the hat and remove only one coin, the unmarked duplicate. No one can tell at a little distance whether it is marked or not, and in any case you immediately place it in the left hand and close the fingers over it.

Bring out a handkerchief and throw it over the fist. As you cover your hand, turn it palm down. Grasp the outside edge of the handkerchief between the thumb and forefinger of your right hand, which you hold palm up. Pull the edge of the handkerchief in toward you and up against the wrist. As the right hand passes beneath the left, let the coin drop into the right hand (fig. 6). (In the photo the near edge of the handkerchief has been lifted to show what happens underneath.)

Ask a spectator to hold the handkerchief around your wrist so that your hand is completely enclosed. Put your right hand into your pocket and bring out a rubber band. Give it to the spectator and ask him to put it over your wrist around the handkerchief.

The trick, as far as you are concerned, is finished. Pretend to pluck an invisible coin from your right hand and throw it toward the hat. Ask the spectator to pull the handkerchief off your hand. Both handkerchief and hand are empty. Don't go near the hat yourself; have someone else go to it and remove the marked coin.

figure 6

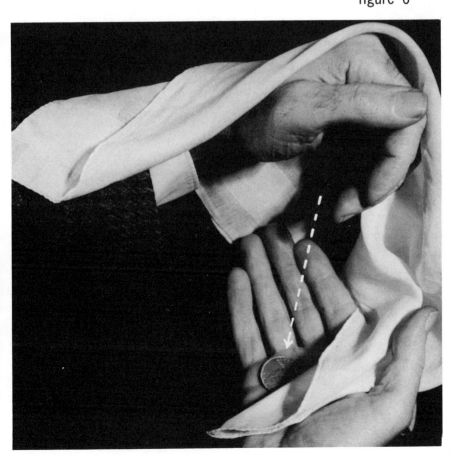

tricky transposition

Two coins, each covered by a handkerchief and each held by
a different spectator, change places on command.

Begin by showing two coins, such as a penny and a nickel,
on the palm of the left hand. Unknown to the audience, your
right hand holds a nickel, which is concealed in the finger-
palm position (fig. 3A).

Throw a handkerchief over your left hand. Pick up the
handkerchief at the center with your right hand, grasping
the two coins through the cloth. What you do now is strictly
for comedy, so speak very seriously.

"*I am going to show you one of the most difficult feats in
all magic. Watch!*" Point your left fingers at the handkerchief and wiggle them in a hypnotic gesture. "*When I do
this, the penny changes into a nickel.*" Reach under the
handkerchief and bring out the nickel. "*And the nickel
changes into a penny!*" Bring out the penny. "*Isn't that won-
derful? Nobody has ever figured out how it works.*

"*And now I'll do something even harder.*" Take the four
corners of the handkerchief with the left hand and let the
center drop. Pick up the penny with the right hand. Place
this hand in the bag formed by the handkerchief (fig. 7).
But instead of leaving the penny inside, as you appear to
do, drop the finger-palmed nickel instead, and push the
penny into the finger-palm position.

Bring the right hand out, hold it under the bag, and grasp
the coin from the outside through the cloth. Drop the four
corners of the handkerchief and turn to a spectator. "*I want
you to hold the penny just like this. Hold it up high so everyone can watch it.*" This instruction is really given so that he
won't open the handkerchief and look inside.

Now hold another handkerchief by the corners, pick up the nickel, and tell another spectator, *"I want you to hold the nickel."* Put it into the bag, but this time leave the penny and retain the nickel. Give this handkerchief to the second spectator to hold.

Reach into your pocket with your right hand, leave the finger-palmed nickel there, and bring out a pencil. The trick is now done and all that remains is to dramatize it.

"Your coin," you ask the second spectator, *"is worth how much more than the other?"* He replies, "Four cents."

"That's correct," you say, *"but when I wave this magic wand* (the pencil) *over your coin, four cents will leave your nickel, fly across the room, and join the penny. If you watch very closely — you won't see a thing. Ready? Go!"*

Each spectator removes his coin, and they find that the penny and nickel have changed places.   **figure 7**

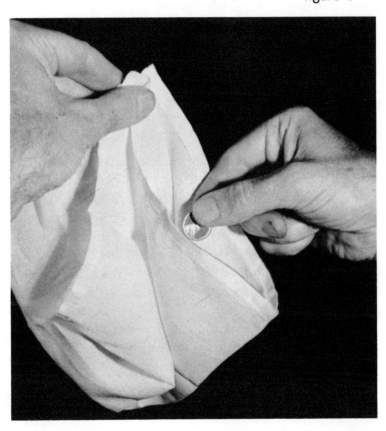

3

SORCERY WITH STRING

through the thumb

A length of string visibly penetrates the performer's thumb.

Loop a length of string over the left thumb as in fig. 8A. Note how the position of the right thumb keeps the string separated. Reach down with the middle finger of the left hand and pull up the lower strand (also fig. 8A). Bring the right hand up and over to the left hand and put the opening above the right thumb over the left thumb (fig. 8B). Now slip the middle finger out of the loop which has formed around it, and then place the left forefinger on the thumb as in fig. 8C.

Give the string a quick tug and it will come free, having apparently passed through the thumb.

figure 8

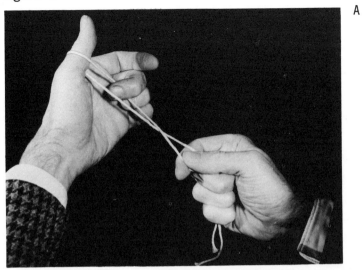

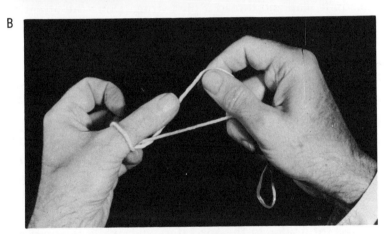

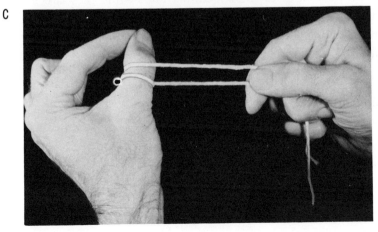

the miraculous match folder

A hole is made in the flap of a match folder with a pencil. A string is threaded through the hole and its ends are held by a spectator, or by two spectators. The performer throws a handkerchief over the match folder, reaches beneath it, and mysteriously removes the folder from the string.

You use two identical match folders. Prepare one in advance by poking a hole in its flap with a pencil. Then conceal it under the band of your wristwatch.

Begin the trick by displaying the duplicate folder, put a hole in its flap and thread it on a string. Don't call attention to the fact verbally, but make sure your audience sees that your hands are empty. Reach under the handkerchief and remove the threaded folder by tearing it. If you make the tear slowly you can do it silently. Push the torn folder down into the left sleeve. Get the duplicate folder from under the watch band and hang it on the string by its flap.

Bring your left hand out and lift the handkerchief up off the string. As soon as the match folder comes into view, your right hand jerks it sharply downward, free of the string. Some spectators will believe that they saw the folder visibly penetrate the string.

Toss the folder to the spectators and, while they are examining it, lower your left arm, let the hidden folder fall into your left hand, and then put it in your pocket together with the handkerchief.

match folder repeat

Spectators will often ask you to repeat the same trick a second time. It is usually not wise to do this and with a trick like the one above, which requires some preparation, you aren't ready to repeat, in any case. But if you can do what seems to be the same trick and use an entirely different method, you can accede to the request and leave your audience twice as mystified as before. Here's a completely different and quite impromptu method of magically removing the match folder from the string.

"This time," you say, *"we'll make it twice as hard. We will double the string."* Actually, as you will see, this makes it twice as easy, but it looks harder.

figure 9

A

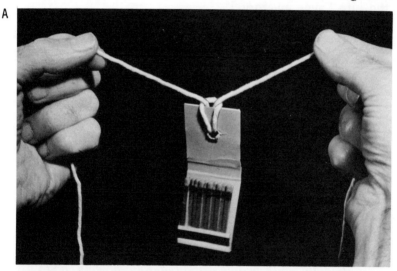

B

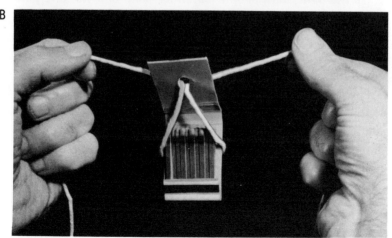

Grasp the string at the center and push the center through the hole in the folder. Then pass both ends of the string through the loop (fig. 9A). Spectators hold the ends of the string and a handkerchief is thrown over the folder.

This time all you need to do is pull the loop out until it is large enough to push the match folder through (fig. 9B). The folder immediately comes free, and has apparently once again penetrated the string. A borrowed key or bracelet can also be removed from the string by this method.

the Life Saver mystery 1

A Life Saver, threaded on a string, is magically removed although both ends of the string are held by spectators.

Cut a Life Saver in half with a razor blade, apply rubber cement to the broken ends, and let it dry. Stick the two halves together again. The join will not be noticeable. Put a duplicate unprepared Life Saver and a handkerchief in your pocket.

Thread the prepared Life Saver on a length of string and have the ends held by spectators. Bring the handkerchief from your pocket, obtaining the second Life Saver at the same time and holding it concealed in the finger-palm position (fig. 3A).

"In the light, with people watching, solid objects can't pass through each other like ghosts. This Life Saver couldn't possibly fall off the string." Cover the Life Saver with the handkerchief. *"But in the dark when no one can see it happen — anything is possible!"*

Place both hands beneath the handkerchief, push a loop of the string through the unprepared Life Saver and over one side, as shown in fig. 10. Separate the two halves of the prepared Life Saver, and conceal them in the finger-palm position in the right hand. Bring both hands into view, lift the

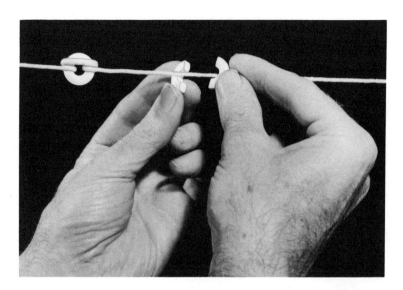

figure 10

handkerchief with the right hand and put it back in your pocket, leaving the prepared Life Saver there at the same time.

"That's odd. The Life Saver went through in the wrong direction and now the string goes through it twice. You can never tell about magic; sometimes it just makes things worse. But a good magician never gives up. Let's try again."

Cover the candy with your fingers, lift the loop over the side of the Life Saver, and then suddenly pull the Life Saver straight down. It comes free. Both it and the string may be examined, because the sole clue to the mystery is safely hidden in your pocket.

the Life Saver mystery 2

If you are asked to perform this trick on some later occasion when you are unprepared, don't let that stop you. Use the following impromptu method.

Open a package of Life Savers, remove several, ask someone to select one and thread it on a string. Put the other Life Savers aside, but steal one and finger-palm it.

This time, under cover of the handkerchief, take the second Life Saver in your left fingers, and encircle the threaded Life Saver and string with your right hand.

Pretend for a moment that you are having trouble, then slide the right hand and the threaded Life Saver out along the string toward its right end. At the same time say, *"Let me hold this end of the string and you hold the Life Saver from the outside through the cloth."*

The Life Saver the spectator holds, is, of course, the unthreaded one. Bring your left hand (palm up) down into view below the handkerchief and tell him to drop the Life Saver at the count of three. It will fall into your hand. Toss it out, lift the handkerchief, and show that there is nothing on the string. Then take the handkerchief in your right hand and pocket it, leaving the other Life Saver there at the same time.

ROPE AND KNOT MAGIC

Rope and knot magic is sure-fire entertainment for an audience of Scouts or Mariners who are learning to tie knots. Since some of these tricks are quick ones that take little time to perform, learn several of them and present them in sequence. The first half dozen tricks that follow have been so arranged that they make up an interesting and surprising routine.

The rope or cord used should be soft and pliable. The best kind is an unwaxed sash cord which may be obtained at any magic shop.

A

figure 11

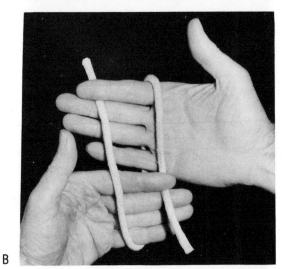

B

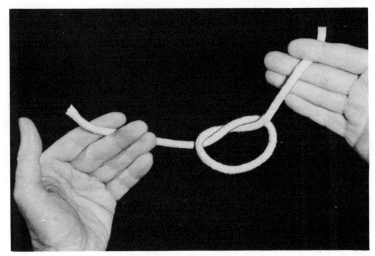

C

the instantaneous knot

A knot is tied instantly.

Hold the rope as shown in fig. 11A. Bring the hands together. The right first and second fingers grasp the left end of the rope, the left first and second fingers grasp the right end (fig. 11B). Pull the hands apart fast. The knot will form at the center (fig. 11C). Bring the hands together and pull them apart as rapidly as possible.

the dissolving knot

Drop the left end of the rope and grasp the knot with the left hand, inserting the first and second fingers into the knot (fig. 12). Bring the right end of the rope over to the knot and hold it between the tips of the left first and second fingers. Immediately take the left end of the rope in the right hand and pull it to the right. The knot will fall off the left fingers and apparently dissolve at the center of the rope.

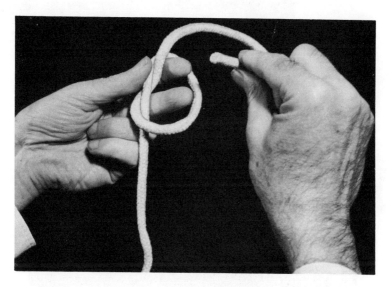

figure 12

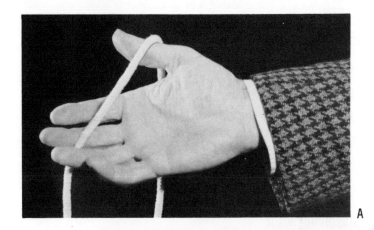

A

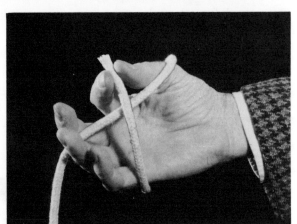

figure 13

B

C

one-hand instant knot

Hold the rope as in fig. 13A. Turn the hand palm down, then lower it quickly and catch the end of the rope that hangs behind the hand with the thumb and forefinger (fig. 13B). Let the loop around the hand fall off, forming a knot (fig. 13C). With a little practice for speed, you will find that a flick of the wrist seems to make the knot form by itself.

the comedy knot

An excellent opener for any series of rope tricks.

Prepare for this in advance by tying a good-sized knot at one end of your rope, then cut it off, and trim both ends close to the knot. Just before you begin the trick, finger-palm this knot in the right hand.

Display a rope about three feet in length and hold it as in fig. 14A. Twist the right fingers inward around the rope and then up behind the left fingers. Grasp the left-hand loop with the right fingers and the right-hand loop with the left fingers (fig. 14B). Pull the hands apart forming a knot (fig. 14C). Pull the knot tight (fig. 14D).

"This is a shoelace knot. And you all know what happens when one or both ends of your shoelaces become entangled in the loops." As you say this, push the right thumb and forefinger in through the loop from the side nearest you, pick up the end of the rope, and pull it through the loop. The left fingers do the same (fig. 14E).

"You get a knot that is extremely difficult to untie." Pull the ends of the rope until the two loops are so small that they become part of the central knot. Don't pull them all the way through because the knot will disappear.

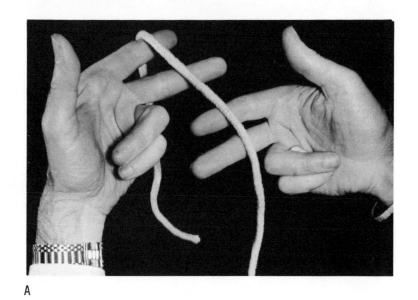

A

figure 14

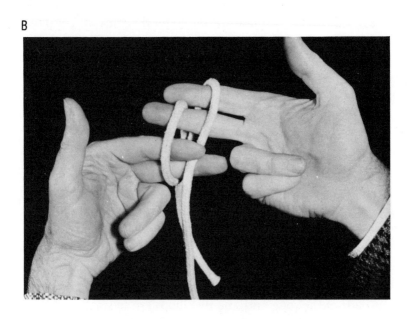

B

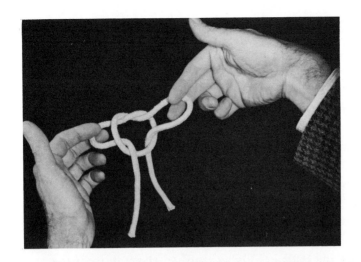

C

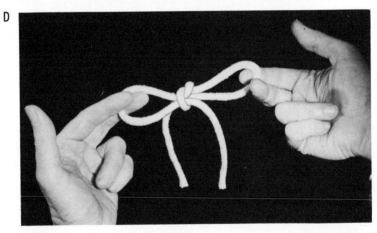

D

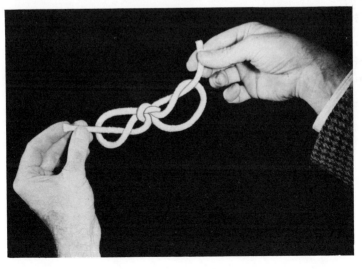

E

Now take both ends of the rope in the left hand. *"Since it is almost impossible to untie this knot the best way to get rid of it is by magic. If I take it in my right hand and pull hard — the knot comes off the rope and I throw it away!"* As you say this, cover the knot with your right fingers and pull. The knot will dissolve in your hand, and you toss the concealed knot to the spectators.

Follow immediately with this. Tie the same knot again, saying, *"I should add a word of warning. When you tie this knot be sure that you don't do this."* Put the ends through the loops as before, but put each end through *twice*. Make certain that the ends are always pushed through from the side away from you; otherwise you'll find that you really do have a knot. Pull, as before, until the loops become part of the central knot.

"If the ends go through the loops twice this gives you the famous Gordian knot which Alexander the Great had to cut. In fact, if there is anyone within the sound of my voice who can untie this knot without cutting the rope I will give him one hundred thousand . . ."

Just as you say *"thousand"* pull the ends of the rope. The knot vanishes. Look at the rope in surprise, then look at the spectators, frown, and add slowly, *"What was I saying?"*

the prisoner escapes

A quick, startling, and seemingly quite impossible escape from a rope tie which Houdini, the greatest of all escape artists, often used.

Rope, cord, or string may be used. Rope is best because it seems more secure and makes the escape look harder. You need two pieces: a short two-foot length and another about ten feet long.

Tell your audience that you are going to enact a TV

Western, all live and in full color. "*I need someone to play the part of Two-Gun Pete, the Terror of the Plains.*" When performing for children don't ever ask for volunteers; you'll be mobbed. Select an assistant and ask him, "*Have you ever had any experience holding up stagecoaches?*" You may get a "yes" to this, because most children know a lot more about this than you do.

Give him the longer rope. "*This is your lasso. Our story starts just as you are holding up the stagecoach. You make one mistake, though. One of the passengers on this coach is Wyatt Earp. That's me.*" (If you're a woman you can be Annie Oakley.) "*But Two-Gun Pete is such a fast man on the draw that he gets the drop on our hero and puts handcuffs on him. The prop man lost the handcuffs that we usually use on this show, but we can make a pair with this short piece of rope. Tie one end around my left wrist.*"

See that he ties several tight knots, the more the better. Have the other end tied around the right wrist in the same way.

"*Now Pete throws one end of his lasso over the handcuffs, takes it again, and then holds both ends tightly*" (fig. 15A).

"*Pete mounts his horse and heads for his hideout in the mountains, with his prisoner walking along behind.*" Have your actor pretend to get on a horse, turn, and move away, his back toward you.

"*Marshal Earp is in a tough spot, because Pete has taken his gun, and the United States Cavalry is two hundred miles away, surrounded by Indians. But Pete, who should know by now that the bad guy never wins, has a surprise coming. When he reaches his hideout and turns around — his prisoner is no longer there!*"

The escape is made during this speech, and at the end of it our hero (you) is still handcuffed, but is free of the lasso.

It's done this way. As you talk, turn your back to the audience, hiding your hands. Grasp the loop of the lasso and

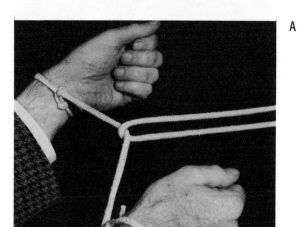

A

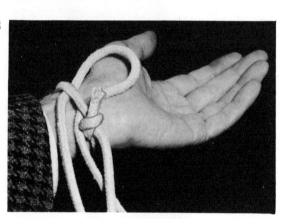

figure 15

B

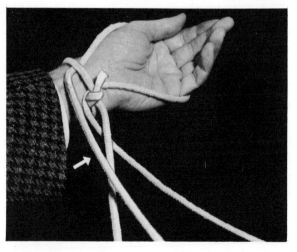

C

push it from the back *under* the circle of rope around the left wrist (fig. 15B). Then pull the loop out and over the left hand (fig. 15C). Grasp the rope at the point indicated by the arrow and pull the loop back under the circle around the wrist again — and you are free. Make the escape as quickly as possible because this makes it obvious that you couldn't have untied and retied the knots. The whole action can be done in a few seconds. As soon as you say, *". . . his prisoner is no longer there!"* drop the lasso and step back. This one escape, because it looks so impossible and is accomplished so quickly, will make your reputation as an escape artist.

When you have learned the foregoing trick you have added three tricks to your repertoire simultaneously. The two that follow, although they look different, are accomplished by exactly the same means.

the mystic ring

The performer's wrists are tied as in the preceding trick, and a rubber Mason jar ring apparently penetrates the rope.

After escaping from the lasso, give the spectator a Mason jar ring. *"Examine that and see if you can find any hole in it."* When he fails, take the ring and say, *"I don't know how you overlooked it. There's quite a large hole in the ring — right through the middle."*

Turn your back, and push one hand through the ring. Slide the ring up the arm, passing it *under* the rope that encircles the wrist (fig. 16A). Then slide the ring down off the hand and over the rope. The ring now encircles the rope between the wrists (fig. 16B). Nothing could be simpler and yet it looks impossible.

Then take the ring off by reversing the procedure, and throw it out for examination.

figure 16

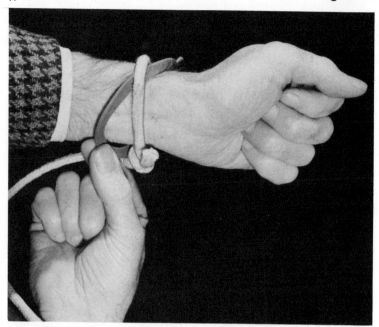

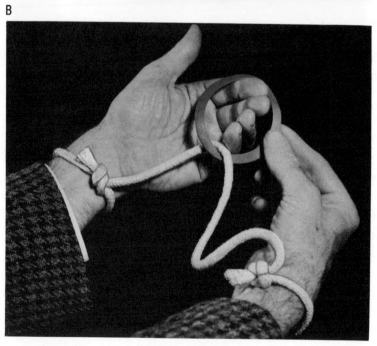

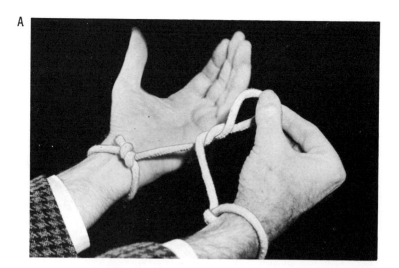

A

figure 17

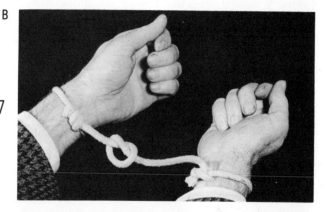

B

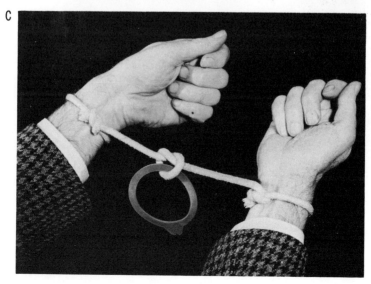

C

the fourth-dimensional knot

A knot can also be tied on the center of the rope between the wrists.

Grasp the rope at the center and give it a triple twist, forming a loop (fig. 17A). Now follow the same procedure as used in freeing yourself of the lasso. Turn your back to the audience. Then push the loop under the rope around the left wrist, over the hand, back down on the outside of the wrist, under the rope again, and then over the hand. This forms a simple overhand knot in the center of the rope (fig. 17B).

If you give the rope an additional twist, the knot formed will be a figure eight.

As a final brain teaser to this series of penetrations, after tying the knot, take the rubber ring again. Place it on the rope as explained in **The Mystic Ring,** then slide it along the rope and into the knot (fig. 17C). This double impossibility seems to prove conclusively that the ring must have penetrated the rope at its center.

the world's most complicated knot

An extremely complicated-looking knot gets smaller and smaller and then vanishes.

Hold both ends of a three-foot rope in your left hand. Put your right hand under and through the loop at the bottom, and grasp both strands of the rope (fig 18A). Pull the rope to the right, forming a double loop (fig. 18B). Push both ends of the rope through both loops (fig. 18C). Take one end in each hand and pull the ends apart until the knot shown in fig. 18D forms.

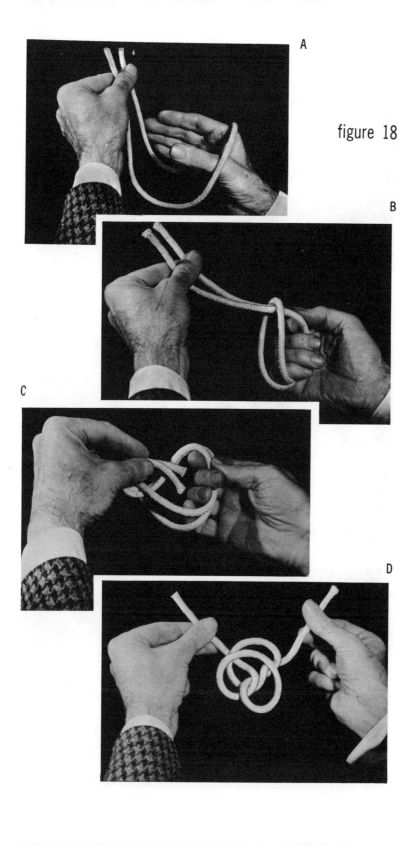

figure 18

A

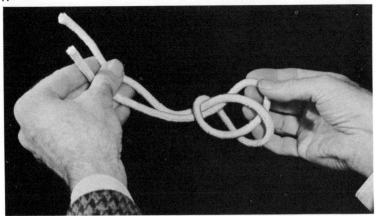

figure 19

B

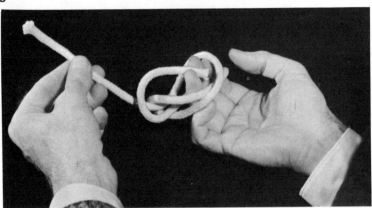

C

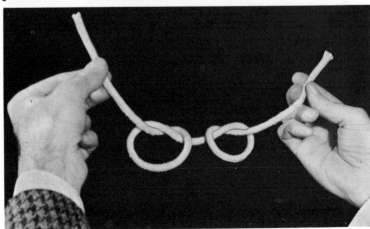

This is all done while you are saying, "*Boys and girls, here is the world's most complicated knot — the double running bowline half-hitch.*"

Now pull the ends apart slowly as you say, "*I spent ten years inventing this knot, but I still haven't found a good use for it.*" The knot gets smaller and smaller and then vanishes. Time this so that the knot vanishes just as you finish speaking.

two knots at once

You apparently tie **The World's Most Complicated Knot** again, but this time you get an entirely different result.

Begin as before (figs. 18A and 18B). Push the loop nearest you through the other loop (fig. 19A). Then put one of the rope ends (the one nearest you in fig. 19A) through both loops (fig. 19B). Pull the ends apart slowly. Two knots will form as in fig. 19C.

visible penetration

A silk scarf visibly penetrates a rope.

Give a spectator a silk scarf, then form a double loop in your rope as in figs. 18A and 18B. Have the spectator thread the scarf through the double loop. Then ask him to tie the ends of the scarf together (fig. 20A). After he has done this, take one end of the rope in each hand and pull the ends apart forcibly with a quick jerk. This causes the rope to become straight, and transfers the double loop to the scarf (fig. 20B).

Give the rope to the spectator and ask him to hold it securely by the ends. "*I am going to try to remove the scarf without touching the knots you tied.*" Grasp the scarf as

A

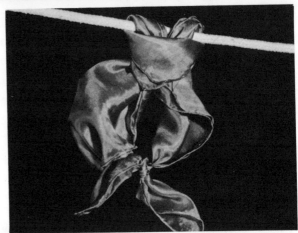

figure 20

B

C

shown in fig. 20C and pull until the knot loosens. Then quickly pull the scarf down and away from the rope. It will appear to pass right through the rope. Display the scarf in a circle, showing that the knots tied by the spectator are still intact, and say, *"Don't ask me how that is done. I have never been able to figure it out myself."*

5

TRICKS WITH EVERYTHING

the rubber band illusion

The most astonishing tricks are those in which the magic happens, not under cover, but in full view. **The Rubber Band Illusion** is one of these. A rubber band visibly penetrates the performer's fingers. It looks like real magic.

Place a rubber band around the first two fingers of the right hand. Put a second rubber band over the first joint of the forefinger, give it a twist, and put it over the second finger, twist it again, put it over the third finger, give it another twist, and put it over the fourth finger, with the result shown in fig. 21A.

Show both sides of the hand to the spectators. *"This first rubber band is not just an ordinary rubber band. It was once owned by a witch. Notice how securely it is fastened on the fingers. All the exits are barred. And yet if I close my fingers*

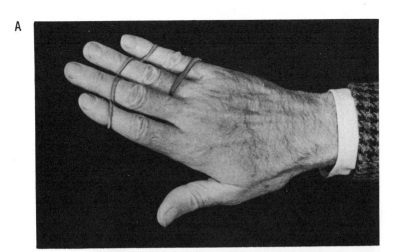

A

figure 21

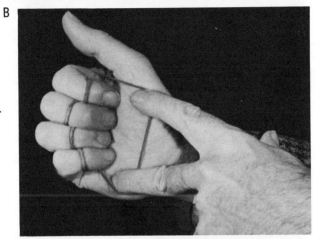

B

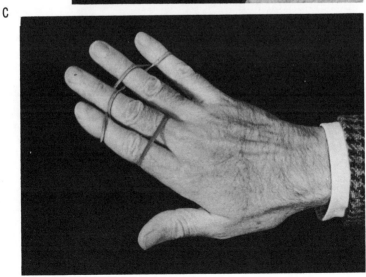

C

and then open them quickly, the magic rubber band passes visibly through all four fingers!"

As you talk, put your left hand under the right one and stretch the hanging loop of the first rubber band so that when you close your fingers, all four finger tips can enter the loop (fig. 21B). This concealed move does the trick. When you open your fingers quickly, the band will jump mysteriously from the first and second fingers over to the third and fourth (fig. 21C).

Repeat the same action and the band will jump back again.

This impossibility may be compounded by using colored rubber bands. Place a red rubber band around the first and second fingers and a green one around the third and fourth fingers. Entwine a third band (of another color) around the finger tips. Now the left hand draws down both colored bands together and all four right fingers enter both bands. Open your fingers quickly and you have two miracles for the price of one. The two bands instantly change places!

This is one of the best of all impromptu tricks; it proves conclusively that you can't believe what you see.

the magnetized knife

A table knife clings to the palm of the magician's hand as though magnetized — then falls when commanded to do so.

The performer explains exactly how this was done, then does it again. This time the spectators see that the explanation given is impossible.

The first explanation is the true one, but the spectators end by doubting it because the magician has switched to a second, different, and better method. The moral: Never trust a magician!

The first method is a simple swindle which takes advantage

of the fact that a pinch of misdirection can prevent a spectator from seeing something that is right in front of his nose.

Begin by holding the left hand palm up and lay the center of the knife on it. Close the fingers around the knife. Now grasp the left wrist with the right hand (fig. 22A). And talk, because what you say provides the needed misdirection. Indirectly, you are telling the audience what to look at so they will overlook something that is plainly visible.

"I squeeze my wrist tightly, shake it a bit, and then turn my left hand over." Relax the right fingers a bit and turn the left hand over so that it is back up. Under the cover of this movement straighten the right finger beneath the left hand and press it against the knife (fig. 22B). Only three of your right fingers are now visible, but if you continue talking about something else, as in the patter given here, this is never noticed.

"When I slowly straighten my fingers, the knife, instead of falling, remains supported by absolutely nothing." (fig. 22C). *"When I say, 'Stop this nonsense!' it hears, obeys, and falls."* Pull the hidden forefinger back a bit and let the knife drop.

Now repeat the trick, but stop while the knife is still suspended and say, *"I'll let you in on a secret — I'm cheating. Apparently none of you can count as far as four. If you could you would have noticed that my right hand now has only three fingers showing. The missing one is here."*

Raise the hands, and let the spectators see how the hidden finger supports the knife. This exposé gets a laugh because they realize how easily they have been fooled.

Now for the double cross. This depends on a secret bit of advance preparation. From the beginning, you have had a long pencil up your left sleeve, held against the inner side of your arm by your wrist-watch band.

At the end of your explanation, let the knife fall and, as the attention of the audience follows it, remove your right

figure 22

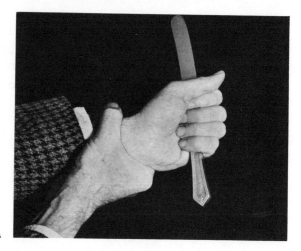

A

hand from your left wrist, grasp the end of the pencil and pull it out so that it extends beneath the palm of your left hand.

"Of course, having spent twenty years in Tibet studying Yoga, I could eliminate the cheating and use real magic, but that's very difficult." No one believes this statement and so you proceed to prove it.

This time your left hand remains palm down throughout. Pick up the knife and place it beneath the left hand, between the palm and the hidden pencil (fig. 22**D**). Close the left fingers around the knife. Grasp the left wrist again, but this time all four fingers can be seen. *"You see. No cheating. All four fingers in view. But if I concentrate hard enough . . ."* Slowly open the left fingers. *". . . the knife doesn't dare fall until I give it my permission. It's scared of me."*

Hold this position a moment, then say, *"All right, knife, that's enough."* Loosen your hold on your wrist and pencil, and the knife falls.

Don't push the pencil back up your sleeve immediately. Wait until they stop watching your hands. Audience attention always scatters just after the climax of a trick. Watch for this and push the pencil up out of sight then.

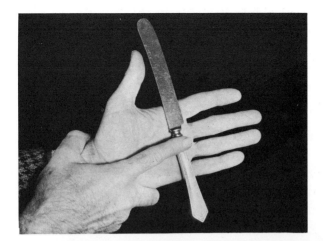

B

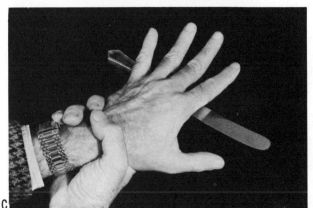

C

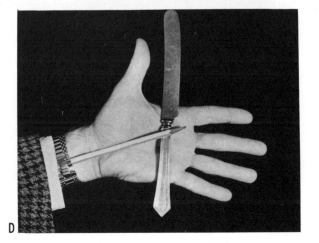

D

egocentric rays

A trick from India. In its original form, a Hindu fakir would ask someone to write his initials on a pebble, throw the pebble into the sacred Ganges River, then hold his hand out, palm toward the water. The fakir would mutter an incantation — and the initials would mysteriously reappear on the hand. You can perform this feat of Indian magic at the dinner table by using a sugar cube instead of a pebble and a glass of water in place of the Ganges.

Ask a spectator to draw a simple geometric figure or print a letter of the alphabet on one side of a sugar lump with a soft lead pencil. While he is doing this, take a drink of water, and leave some moisture on the outside of the rim of the glass. Then moisten the ball of your thumb by passing it over the damp glass rim.

Take the sugar lump and show everyone the pencil mark. Pick up the glass of water with your other hand and place it before a spectator. This action will divert attention away from the sugar. At the same time, turn the sugar lump in your fingers and press your moistened thumb on the mark. The thumb will pick up a reverse image of the mark.

Now drop the sugar (mark up) into the water and have the spectator cover the mouth of the glass with his hand. "No," you say then, "that's not quite right." Lift his hand off the glass, and move the glass slightly as though its exact position was of great importance. This misdirection serves to keep attention on the glass so that your audience does not notice that you are holding the spectator's hand with your thumb beneath it and pressed against his palm. This unseen action leaves the mark on his hand.

Replace his hand on the glass, then call attention to the

small air bubbles from the sugar. *"Those bubbles contain egocentric rays which have a curious action. Notice how they take the particles of graphite from the sugar and carry them up to the surface of the water."*

Wait until the mark on the sugar has dissolved, then add, *"The egocentric rays, through some mysterious electrochemical process still unexplained by science, redeposit all those particles of graphite in the same pattern on your hand."*

This is nonsensical and yet — when the spectator turns his hand over he finds the mark on his palm. The time interval and the misdirection in what you have been saying makes him forget that you ever touched his hand. Some spectators will half believe the egocentric-ray theory you have suggested and will try the experiment for themselves. When it fails, as it always does, you say, *"Apparently you're not egocentric enough."*

Here's a variation which is even more inexplicable because the spectator himself drops the sugar into the water and you never touch it at all. You have a second sugar lump and another pencil which you place in your lap before you begin the trick. While the spectator is drawing his mark on his sugar lump, you secretly duplicate it on your own. Your moistened thumb picks up this duplicate impression, and, after the spectator drops his sugar lump into the glass, you transfer your mark to his palm.

the linking clips

Two paper clips link themselves together in a curious fashion. Every child wants to learn to do a trick and this is one you can teach them and which they can do immediately.

Fold one-third of the length of a dollar bill inward. Fold the other end outward. The upper edge of the bill now has the shape of the letter S. Put two paper clips on the upper

figure 23

edge of the bill (fig 23). One clip holds the left end of the bill and the center section together. The other joins the right end of the bill and the center section.

When you pull the ends of the bills in opposite directions the paper clips jump off the bill and link together.

The stunt can be seen more easily by a group if you use a chain of a dozen or more clips linked together. Have two spectators hold the opposite ends of the chain. Unlink two clips in the center of the chain and attach them to the bill. Now, when you pull on the bill, the clips link and the two halves of the chain are rejoined.

the surprise penetration

A dinner-table trick with a real surprise ending.

Fold a paper napkin and place a drinking glass on it as

shown in fig. 24A, page 66. Roll the glass forward, wrapping it in the paper. Twist the ends of the paper at the bottom of the glass so that the paper will remain in position.

Place a coin on the table. *"I am going to make the coin pass down through the table top. Since this can only be done in the dark, we must cover the coin."* Lay a folded paper napkin on the coin and then place the paper-covered glass on both, mouth down.

Make whatever magic passes and intone whatever incantation you like, then pick up the covered glass and bring it back to the edge of the table. Ask someone to lift the napkin and see if the coin has gone.

As everyone watches this operation, allow the glass to slide out of its paper cover and down into your left hand which is ready to receive it (fig. 24B).

When the coin is seen to be still there, ask someone to turn it over on the excuse that it is wrong-side-up. Then have the napkin replaced. Put the glass on it again (actually only the paper cover). Start to make another magic pass, then say, *"Wait, I just thought of an even better trick."* Drop your left hand to your lap, get the glass and reach out under the table with it. *"I'll make the glass go through the table instead."* Smack your hand solidly down on the paper cover, squashing it flat. Then bring the glass from under the table.

This unexpected finale is a real surprise.

If you use an unbreakable plastic glass, place it between your knees just after it has dropped from its cover. Then bring your left hand above the table. Now, when you flatten the paper cover, spread your knees and let the glass fall to the floor.

through the table

Three paper balls pass magically through a table top and a fourth flies invisibly from one place to another.

A

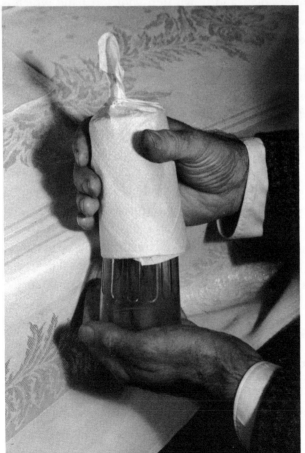

figure 24

B

Tear a paper napkin into quarters and crumple each piece into a ball. Lay them out on a table about a foot and a half apart, forming a square. Show two men's hats, letting the spectators see that both are empty. Hold them by the brims with your fingers inside the hats.

Now, as in many tricks, you proceed promptly to get one jump ahead of the spectators and stay that way throughout. First, put the hat you hold in your right hand down over the ball on the right. As you do this, extend the first and second fingers beneath the hat and clip the ball between them.

Then bring the hat you hold in your left hand over to the right so that it is directly above and covers the right hand as it comes out from under the first hat with the ball (fig. 25A).

Your right hand takes this hat and your left hand goes at once, taking the attention of the audience with it, to the second paper ball, which it picks up for a moment and then replaces. Your right hand now covers this ball with the hat and leaves the concealed ball there also.

From the spectator's viewpoint the trick is just beginning; actually, with this one secret move, you are practically done. Pick up one of the remaining balls with your right hand, carry it down under the table, and rap your knuckles against the underside of the table as you say, *"Go!"*

Lift the hat on your left by the crown with the left hand, showing the two balls. Bring the hat back to the table edge so that it covers your right hand, which comes out from under the table with the ball it still holds and takes the hat by the brim (fig. 25B).

Repeat the same action. Cover the two visible balls with the hat and add the third one. Pick up the last ball with the right hand, put it under the table, command it to go, and lift the hat, showing three balls.

Again, transfer the hat from the left to the right hand just as the latter comes out from under the table. Drop the hat on the three balls, adding the fourth.

You are all set for the climax. Point to the hat on the right and say, *"Now I'll make the first ball fly invisibly through the air and through both hats to join the other three. Watch!"* Snap your fingers. Stand back and ask the spectators to lift the hats themselves.

Practice this trick before trying it on anyone, so that you can do all the moves without hesitation. When done smoothly, it is highly effective and very mystifying.

figure 25

A

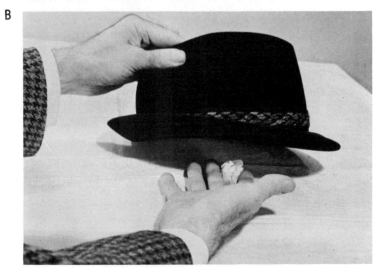

B

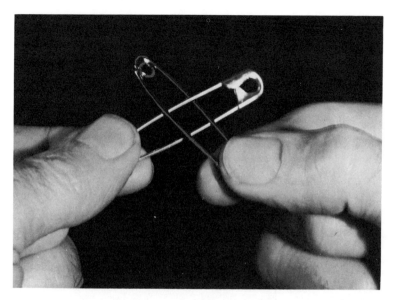

figure 26

soft steel

Two safety pins, linked together, are separated without being opened, one apparently passing visibly through the other.

Link the two pins and hold them exactly as shown in fig. 26. Note the pin held by the right hand. The bar which opens is at the top, and this bar is the only one which lies *above* the bars of the other pin at the intersections where they cross.

Blow on the pins, explaining, *"This softens the steel."* Then quickly jerk both hands apart. The pins separate, although still closed. Since there are several other starting positions, all of them wrong, anyone else who tries the feat is unlikely to succeed.

the message from the ashes

The performer tells a story about a King and his Court Magician in which the magic happens as the story is told. We give the story first, the method at the end.

Once upon a time there was a King who had a large family of Princes and Princesses. Like all parents, the King was a little bit crazy and thought that the Princes and Princesses should help do some of the chores around the castle. One chore that they all hated was emptying the wastebaskets. Nobody knows why. Maybe it was because there were 116 rooms in the castle and 198 wastebaskets.

"I don't know what to do," the King told the Prime Minister. "Every time I tell one of those kids that if he doesn't empty the wastebaskets I'll chop off his head he runs away and hides under a bed. I can't spend all day looking under the 95 beds in this castle; it wouldn't be dignified. The situation is serious. Do you think I should call out the Army?"

"You can't," the Prime Minister said. "The Army is on vacation. But I have a scheme. We will put the kids' names in a hat. Then you issue a Royal Decree announcing that there will be a drawing for a prize every morning."

"Maybe I am thick-headed," said the King, "but I don't see how giving away prizes will solve the wastebasket problem."

"Why not, your Majesty? The child whose name is drawn must empty the wastebaskets. That's the prize and kids love prizes."

The King thought about this for a minute, and then turned to the Captain of the Guards. "We must give the Prime Minister a suitable reward for his suggestion. Turn him over to the Chief Executioner and have his head chopped off. The Princes and Princesses would all be mad at me if I tried such a mean underhanded scheme. Besides, I don't want to make people mad at me while the Army is on vacation."

But the wastebasket problem got worse every day. In fact, the gold wastebasket in the throne room became so filled with old Royal Decrees, bills, and chewing-gum wrappers that the King received a warning from the fire department saying that if something was not done about it they would have to close the palace and board up all the windows.

The King *had* to do something. So he tried the Prime Minister's scheme anyway. He got all the Princes and Princesses together and wrote the name of each one on a separate slip of paper. He mixed the papers in a hat and had one drawn. But the Princes and Princesses suspected the King was up to no good and they wouldn't show him the slip which had been drawn.

The poor King didn't know what to do so he called for the Court Magician. "You find out who won the prize," he ordered. "And hurry, or I'll have your head chopped off, too. I'm beginning to get angry."

"Oh, that's easy," the Magician said. "We'll just look at all the names left in the hat and see which one is missing." But while he was saying this one of the princes grabbed all the other slips and burned them.

This made the King really angry. He roared, "I have a good notion to chop off everybody's head!"

"No," the Magician said, "Don't do that. I'll use some magic."

He rolled up his sleeve, took the ashes of the burned papers, muttered a secret incantation, rubbed the ashes on his arm — and the missing name appeared magically!

In advance, cut a narrow piece from one end of a bar of soap. Moisten one end and use it to print the name of one of the spectators on your arm. Another method is to use a strong soap solution and write the letters in script with an artist's water-color brush. When dry, the lettering will be invisible.

When you tell how the King wrote the names on slips of paper, produce a pad and pencil and do the same. Hold the pad so that the spectators cannot see what you write, and tear off each slip, fold it, and drop it into a hat. Ask each child for his first name, then pretend to write it, but actually write the *same name* each time — the one which is lettered on your arm.

Do this with all the slips except one. On this slip, write the name called, then show it to the spectators on the pretense that you want to make sure you have spelled the name correctly. When you drop this slip into the hat, put it to one side, separated from the others. After all the slips are in, reach into the hat, take the odd slip in your fingers, and mix up the others. Then hold the hat by the brim, your fingers inside and covering the odd slip. Ask a spectator to draw one slip from the hat, and tell him not to open it until the end of the story.

When you reach the point in the story where the papers are burned, take all the remaining slips (including the odd one) out of the hat, and burn them in an ashtray. As you finish the story, roll up your sleeve, take the ashes in your hand, and rub them briskly on your arm. The carbonized ash will stick to the soap and the invisible letters will appear magically (fig. 27).

Ask the spectator who drew the slip to open it and read the chosen name aloud.

figure 27

6

SELF-WORKING CARD TRICKS

the mystic fifteen

The spectator merely thinks of a card and the performer finds it.

Deal out three piles of five cards each. Ask someone to choose any pile, look at the cards in it, and mentally select one. Sandwich the spectator's cards between the other two piles. Now, from this pile of fifteen cards, deal off five cards in a row. Deal another card onto each of these five cards, working from left to right, and then a third card on each pile.

Ask the spectator to find the pile that contains his card and place it in his pocket. *"Remember,"* you tell him, *"that you selected a card merely by thinking of it. Now think of the name again."* Touch his forehead with your fingers while he is thinking, as if picking up the vibrations. Then reach into his pocket and remove one face-down card. Don't look at it.

"That's not yours." Bring a second card from his pocket. *"And it's not that one. Name your card, please. And let us see what you have in your pocket."* The single remaining card is the mentally selected one.

The selected card will always be the middle card of the three, so you merely remove the first and third.

instant hypnotism

A spectator chooses one of two piles of playing cards and, without fail, selects the one the performer has predicted he will choose. This is a barefaced but puzzling swindle.

The performer places two small packets of cards before a spectator, then writes something on a slip of paper, folds it, and lets the spectator hold it.

"I have just written something I want you to do. Some children never seem to want to do what they are told, but I have a way to fix that. I hypnotize them — like this." Look the spectator in the eyes and snap your fingers. *"There! You're hypnotized, and this is such a good brand of hypnotism that you don't even know it. But I'll prove it. Just touch either one of those piles of cards, and remember — the paper you hold tells which pile you will touch. No matter how hard you try you won't be able to touch the other one. It's absolutely impossible. Just try it. Touch one."*

When he does, say, *"That one? Are you sure? Would you change your mind if I gave you the chance? You can, if you like. No? All right, open the paper and read what I wrote."*

The prediction reads: "You will choose the six pile."

You can't lose. It doesn't matter which pile is chosen nor how often he changes his mind. One pile contains four sixes, the other contains six cards. If he chooses the first, turn the cards face up and spread them, showing that they are all sixes. Then show that there are no sixes in the other pile. If he chooses the other pile, don't show the faces. Simply pick up the chosen pile and count them face down, showing that there are six cards. Spread the remaining pile, showing only four cards.

the lazy magician

The magician never touches the cards but succeeds in finding the one the spectator is thinking of. There is no preparation. Just follow the procedure below and it works automatically.

Give the deck to a spectator and then turn your back. *"Take a dozen or so cards and put the rest of the deck aside. Shuffle the cards thoroughly. When you have finished, look at the bottom card and remember it. And show it to the rest of the audience so they can help you remember it."* This last instruction is always good. It insures that the person who chose the card won't ruin your climax by forgetting it.

"Now select a number between one and ten — any number at all — and transfer that many cards from the top of the pile to the bottom. Since I don't know that number, your card, as far as I am concerned, is lost." Turn and face the audience.

"Next, deal the cards face down into a pile, one at a time. Keep thinking of your card and I'll try to stop you when you come to it."

Pretend to concentrate but let the spectator deal all the cards without stopping him. Shake your head. *"You're not concentrating hard enough. I didn't get a thing. Let's go back a bit. Take the same number as before and transfer that many cards from top to bottom."* Turn away as this is being done so you can't see how many cards are moved.

When he has done this, the remembered card will always

be the top card of the packet he holds. But don't stop here; continue as before.

"*Deal the cards again one at a time and keep thinking of your card.*" Watch the deal, mentally count the cards, and after he has dealt, say, five cards, stop him.

"*Wait! You've gone past it. Put those cards back on the deck and deal again slowly.*"

If you stopped the deal after five cards were dealt you now know that the chosen card is now fifth from the top. So on this deal, as he takes off the fifth card, say, "*Stop! Name your card!*"

He does this, and when he looks at the card he holds he finds that it is his.

automatic detection

The performer finds a card on which the spectator is concentrating without ever seeing the faces of any of the cards. The feat appears to be quite impossible but the method is as simple as they come. It works automatically.

Let a spectator shuffle the deck and ask him to think of a number between one and twenty-five. Turn your back and tell him to deal that many cards from the deck into a face-up pile. Caution him to do it silently so that you get no clue as to the number.

When he says that he has finished, tell everyone to remember the card on the top of the face-up pile. Ask the spectator to turn the dealt cards face down and replace them on the deck.

Face your audience again and take the deck. "*I am going to try to find the card you are thinking of without looking at any of the cards and while the deck is behind my back. You must all help by concentrating on the card as hard as you can.*"

Hold the deck behind your back, turn it face up, and mentally select a number of your own — ten, let us say. Count this many cards off the face of the deck and put them under the others. Then shake your head and tell the spectators, *"You are obviously not concentrating very hard. The thought waves I'm getting are much too faint for any good use."*

Give the deck back to the spectator. *"But I never give up. We'll do it a bit differently. Deal off the same number of cards you dealt before, but face down this time so I can't see any of them."* Turn away as he does this.

When he says he has finished, face him again, and tell him to continue dealing. Mentally count the cards as they are dealt. If the number of cards you moved from the face to the top of the deck behind your back was ten, then the chosen card is now the tenth card down. Stop the deal when the count reaches nine and have the chosen card named.

The spectator turns the next card face up and finds that it is the one he selected.

the spectator does a trick

For a change, the magician chooses a card and the spectator finds it!

Select a spectator to assist you and tell him, *"Magic is very difficult work and I'm tired. This time, I will choose a card and let you be the magician and do the magic."*

Count off twenty cards, hand them to your assistant and ask him to shuffle them. *"Now spread the cards so I can choose one."* Take a card and look at it, making sure that the "magician" doesn't see what it is. For that matter, make sure no one else sees it either, because you are merely acting and this card has nothing to do with the trick at all. Push the card back among those the "magician" holds and tell him to shuffle them thoroughly.

Children always hope to be able to outwit you and most of them will shuffle so long that you have to put a stop to it. *"Remember,"* you say, *"that you are the one who is going to have to find that card. Aren't you making it a bit tough?"* When he finally agrees that the shuffling has been completed, ask, *"Do you know what my card is? And do you have the faintest idea where it is?"* He admits he is totally in the dark.

"Good. Now since you probably don't trust me at all, I'll write down the name of my card so that there can't be any argument about it later." Take out pencil and paper and start to write.

Then stop. *"This is a pretty kettle of fish! People are always forgetting their cards when I do tricks — and now I've done it!"*

Reach out, take the cards, look at the faces very quickly. Get a look at and remember the top card. *"Oh, yes. Now I remember."*

Write the name of the top card on your paper, fold it and give it to someone to hold.

Turn to the "magician" and say, *"One of the best ways to find a card whose name you don't know is to call out the first number you think of between one and ten. Try that."*

It doesn't matter what number he calls; any one will do. If he calls *six* tell him to deal off six cards, one at a time, and turn the last one face up. Be sure he deals them one at a time; this is important because it reverses the order of the dealt cards and puts the top one where you want it.

Scowl at the card he turns up. *"Maybe that isn't the best way to do this after all. That's not my card. Please replace those cards on the others. We'll try something else."* Turn to another spectator. *"You look psychic. Perhaps you can do better. Give us a number between eleven and twenty. Higher numbers are usually better anyway."*

Again it doesn't matter what number is called. Suppose it is seventeen. Tell the "magician" to deal off sixteen cards one at a time and turn up the seventeenth. *"That,"* you say, *"is still not my card."* Have him turn it down again and replace the dealt cards on the others.

Say, *"I can't understand why this doesn't work. Let's try something different. Let's take that first wrong number and subtract it from the second wrong number. Maybe that will work. Six from seventeen is eleven. Deal ten cards and turn up the eleventh."*

This will be the right one, but look at it dubiously. *"Do you know I've forgotten my card again? It's a good thing I wrote it down."* Ask the spectator who holds the paper to open it and read aloud what he finds there. Tell the "magician," *"I thought for a minute that you were never going to make it, but you did fine. You won't tell anyone how you did that, will you?"*

find it yourself

A spectator performs a card trick himself without knowing how he did it.

Tell a spectator that you will teach him how to be a magician in one easy lesson. Give him a deck of cards to shuffle, then ask him to return about half the deck to you. *"Since you are going to do this trick without any help from me, I'll turn my back so that I can't see what happens and can't help you."* Face the other way and instruct him to cut the cards he holds several times. Then tell him to look at and remember the top card and replace it face down on top.

While he is doing this, hold your cards close to your body so that no one behind you can see them and keep your elbows pressed against your sides so that there is no telltale movement. Without looking down at the deck, turn the bottom card face up under the deck. Then lift the top card, turn the second card from the top face up, and replace the top card. Square the deck neatly.

When the spectator says he is ready, face him. Put your cards on those he has, saying, *"We'll bury your card in the deck. Now put the deck behind your back and face the audience. You are now going to try to find your card while the deck is behind your back and in less than three seconds. Are you sure you can do that?"* The answer is bound to be "No."

"Don't say that. If you really believe you can do it, you will. A magician has to have self-confidence. It's impossible, of course, but it's not really hard. Take the top card from the deck and give it to me so I can show you just what to do."

Hold the card he gives you face down and instruct him, *"Take the next card off the top of the deck and turn it over face up, like this."* Turn your card over. *"Then push it face up into the center of the deck. Nothing hard about that, was there? Now give me the deck."*

Place the deck on the table or floor and spread it out. One face-up card shows in the center. This is the card you secretly reversed on the bottom of the deck earlier, but the spectator thinks it is the card he just reversed.

"Now let's look at the card just below the one you inserted." Remove the card below the face-up card. Ask the spectator to name his card and then turn over the card you hold.

"Congratulations! You did it on the very first try!"

the secret number

Clairvoyance is the faculty of obtaining information directly by the mind without the use of any of the senses. This trick, a guaranteed baffler, will convince anyone that you have that ability. The performer never touches the cards at any time and the trick works itself.

Have a spectator shuffle the deck, then say, *"I'll turn my back so that I can't see anything you do. Please cut a few cards off the top of the deck. Not too many; otherwise the trick will take too long. Then count the cards you removed. Count them silently so I can't hear what is happening. Remember the number, and put the counted cards out of sight in your pocket.*

"You now have, buried in your mind, a secret number that no one else can possibly know. Now count down from the top of the deck to that number, look at the card at that number, and remember it. Leave the card at that position, and square the deck."

Turn and face the spectator. *"I want you to begin dealing cards, one at a time, from the top of the deck face down into a pile on the table. I am sure you will admit that I can't possibly know the name or location of your card. I have seen nothing, heard nothing, and know nothing; yet I will attempt the completely impossible feat of stopping the deal when you have your chosen card in your hand. Put on your best poker face and make sure you give me no clues. Now deal. Not too fast, please. And don't stop until I ask you to."*

Place one hand to your forehead, as if concentrating, and cover your eyes almost completely, but not so much that you can't surreptitiously see below the hand and watch the cards as they are dealt. You want this deal to go *beyond* the chosen card, and, since you asked him to cut off a small number, he probably took less than fifteen cards.

Mentally count the cards as they are dealt and stop him after fifteen have been dealt. *"I think I missed your card. I have gone past it, haven't I?"* If he says, "Yes," you are all set.

If he says "No," ask him to continue dealing and stop him after another half dozen cards have been dealt. Continue your mental count. Ask the same question again. Repeat, if necessary, until he admits that you have gone past his card.

Be sure to remember how many cards have been dealt; this is the secret clue you need.

"*This is such a difficult feat that I think I'll have to go into a trance. Put the cards back on the deck and we'll try once more.*"

After he replaces the cards, add, "*Let's make it even tougher and lose your card even more thoroughly in the deck. Put the cards in your pocket back on the deck, too.*" This last instruction is what does the trick. Although you never discover the original number that was selected, you now know the exact location of the chosen card.

Have him begin to deal again. Count the cards. If the number dealt on the previous deal was fifteen, let him deal fifteen cards and stop him just as he picks up the sixteenth. He must always deal the *same* number of cards as he did on the previous deal, whatever it was — and you stop him on the next following card. This card will be the chosen one.

Have him name his card first, then turn it face up. This is about as close as you can come to real clairvoyance.

the reluctant card

A selected card, lost in the deck, reveals itself in an odd way.

Shuffle the deck. Then, as you step toward a spectator, begin running the cards from the left to the right hand. Mentally count them as you do so. Feed them across as rapidly as you can, counting by feel, and without looking at them. If you do this in an easy, natural way no one will realize that you are counting.

Ask the spectator to take a card whenever he likes. When he removes one, keep the cards in the right hand (which you have counted) slightly separated from the rest of the deck.

Turn your back and tell him to look at the card, remember it, and show it to the others.

While your back is turned, continue counting the cards until you reach twenty-one. Face the spectators again, separate the deck below the twenty-first card and have the chosen card replaced between the two packets.

If the spectator is slow to take a card, and you reach the count of twenty-one before he has done so, simply retain a slight break in the spread of cards at that point and continue pushing cards across, without counting, until one is selected. Then, when your back is turned, separate the deck at the break so that your right hand holds only twenty-one cards.

Square the deck and give it the false cut explained on page 99 so that no one will suspect that the card is being controlled in a certain location.

"One doesn't really need to be a magician to do card tricks. If you concentrate on your card hard enough, sometimes it will find itself. Let's try it."

Quickly deal all the cards into two piles as though you were about to play a two-handed game. Always deal the spectator the first card.

"Look at the cards you have and see if yours is there." He looks and does not find it. *"We'll discard those cards and try again."*

Deal the remaining cards into two new piles. Again the chosen card is not found among those the spectator receives and he again discards his pile. This is repeated until, on the last deal, the spectator receives only two cards, neither of which are his.

The performer holds only one card, and this proves to be the chosen one.

Note: be sure to use a full deck of fifty-two cards.

multiple reverse

On command a number of chosen cards simultaneously turn face up.

"Would anyone," you ask, *"like to learn how to do a trick?"* Every child in the audience will undoubtedly raise his hand and holler, "Me!" If you are performing for a small group of five or six say, *"Okay, you can all try it."* If the audience is larger, use five or six spectators in the front row.

Shuffle the deck as you go forward, then spread the cards and ask the first spectator to take one. *"But don't look at it yet. Hold it face down."* Have each of the others also take a card. Then turn your back and tell them all to look at their cards, remember them, and turn them face down again so that you won't be able to see any of them.

While your back is toward the spectators, turn the deck face up and then turn the top card face down. Keep the deck neatly squared so that you seem to be holding a face-down deck.

Now go to the first spectator, take his face-down card from him and push it into the deck — not too far from the top. Do the same with each of the other chosen cards in the order in which they were selected, replacing each one a bit farther down in the deck. Keep the deck neatly squared throughout, so that none of the face-up cards show. Don't use a deck with an all-over back design; use one that has white margins.

Now ask the first spectator to step forward and assist you. As he does so, lower your left hand (which holds the deck) to your side momentarily. Then bring it up in front of your body again, *palm down,* and transfer the deck to your right hand. This action has casually and surreptitiously turned the deck over.

Tell the assisting spectator, *"Now we'll see how good a magician you are."* Replace the deck in your left hand and keep it tilted forward a bit so that no one can see the bottom card faces the wrong way. *"Name your card aloud and command it to turn over."* Criticise his manner of doing this. *"You must speak louder. I don't think the card could hear that."* And remind him he forgot to snap his fingers. Have him do it again. *"That's much better. It might even work."*

Then either have each child in turn command his card to turn over or have them all do it at once. *"Now, let's see how many of you were successful."*

Ask the first spectator to name his card again, and then begin pushing the cards off the top of the deck into the left hand. When the first face-up card appears, lift off all the cards above it and give them to the assisting spectator to hold. Lift the face-up card, show it and compliment the spectator on his magic powers.

Replace it face down on the deck, ask the second spectator to name his card, and push over more cards until this one also appears face up.

Each time give the pushed-off cards to your assistant to hold, and be sure to keep the cards in your left hand well squared throughout so that they always cover the bottom face-up card and it is not seen.

When the last chosen card has been found and shown, congratulate the spectators. *"You all do that very well; I'm amazed. I hope that you are all as well trained as these cards, and obey orders from your parents just as promptly."*

The audience participation makes this one of the most entertaining card tricks you can do.

Retrieve the cards the assisting spectator holds and replace them on the cards you have left. The single face-up card on the bottom of the deck must be secretly reversed again at the first opportunity. Even better, leave the card face up, and perform **The Upside-down Miracle,** which follows. Since it makes use of a face-up bottom card, you are all set for it.

the upside-down miracle

The two halves of a deck of cards are placed face to face, and all the cards mysteriously turn face down on command.

Before beginning, secretly reverse the bottom card of the deck so that it is face up. If you do this trick immediately after the **Multiple Reverse,** the bottom card is already in that position.

"These are probably the best-trained cards in captivity. Watch them now as they perform a completely impossible feat of acrobatics!"

Bring your right hand above the deck, grasp it at the ends, and cut off half the cards (fig. 28A). Then, *simultaneously and quickly,* turn your right hand palm up and your left hand palm down (fig. 28B). At the same time say, *"I turn half the deck face up and place it on the bottom."* Put the cards in your right hand *under* those in your left hand and square the deck.

"The two halves face each other." Turn the deck over three times showing backs on both sides. Actually, all the cards now face the same way except for one, which, after the third turn, is on the bottom.

Pull the bottom card out from beneath the deck. *"If I take one of the face-up cards and wave it gently over the others, all the cards mysteriously and invisibly turn face down!"*

Drop the single card face down on the others. Then run all the cards from hand to hand, showing that they are all face down. This is a quick trick but a startling one.

x-ray vision

A spectator cuts a deck into three piles. The performer claims

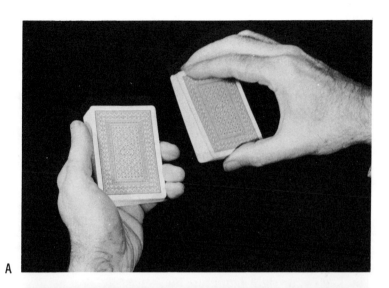

A

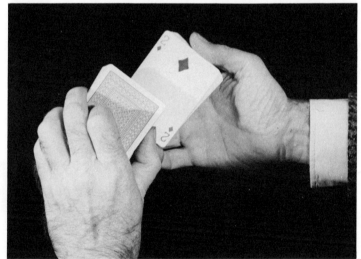

B

figure 28

he has X-ray vision, and apparently proves this by naming the card on the bottom of each pile.

Have the deck shuffled, and secretly glimpse the bottom card as you take the deck and place it on the table. Ask someone to cut it into three piles. We'll call the piles A, B, and C. You know the name of the card at the bottom of pile A because it formed the lower portion of the deck.

Gaze intently at pile C and announce that its bottom card is the ——— of ———. (Name the card you know.) Pick up pile C, your right thumb at the inner end, fingers at the outer end, and bring it back to your left hand. As it comes back, tip it up just enough so that you get a quick passing glance at the bottom card (fig. 29). Try this a few times and you'll find that you need only the briefest of glimpses to identify the card. The slight tilting up of the packet won't be noticed if you keep your right hand moving.

Pull off the bottom card with the fingers of the left hand and put the pile back where it was.

Turn your X-ray vision on pile B, and name the card you just glimpsed. Then pick up pile B, again sighting the bottom card. Pull the bottom card off onto the card already in your left hand. Do the same with pile A, except that you do

figure 29

not need to glimpse the bottom card. Place pile A *below* rather than above the two cards in your left hand so that when the bottom card is pulled off it lies beneath the other two. This puts the cards in the proper sequence.

Turn the three cards toward yourself, name the card facing you again, and deal it off, face up, onto pile C. Do the same with the others, putting them on piles B and A.

Do the whole trick rather quickly and then proceed to something else. If you are asked to do it again, do it later, not right away.

cherchez la femme

An easy non-sleight-of-hand version of the famous Three Card Monte swindle with a surprise finish. You use it, not as a swindle, but as an observation or alertness test which looks dead easy but which no one ever passes.

One bit of secret preparation before you begin: Place a red Queen face up on the top of the face-down deck, and cover it with any other card, face down.

"Did you know," you begin, *"that a great many people walk in their sleep? They go around that way for days sometimes and never know it."* Select one spectator. *"You, for instance. Are you quite certain that you are really wide awake? You are? I'm not so sure about that. I'd like to give you a test to find out."*

Turn the deck face up and run through the cards. Find and throw out another red Queen and the two Aces. Keep the last few cards on the bottom of the face-up deck squared so that the reversed Queen won't be seen.

"Can you identify these three cards?" The spectator names them. *"Very good. You seem to be partly awake."*

While the attention is on the spectator, square the deck, turn it face down and tilt it toward yourself. Slide the top card off and place it on the bottom of the deck. Don't try to hide this action, just do it casually. Then slide the face-up Queen (now on top of the deck) down so that it projects over the inner edge of the deck about a half inch (fig. 30).

Tell the spectator, *"Your job is to try and keep your eye on this odd card."* Point to the face-up Queen on the table. *"In fact, keep both eyes on it — and keep them both wide open."*

Pick up either Ace and put it, face up, on the deck, directly on the face-up Queen already there. Run your right thumb along the lower edge of the two cards to line them up exactly.

Pick up the Queen on the table, and place it on the Ace at an angle so that the index of the Ace is still visible. Put the last Ace on the Queen in the same way.

"Please notice that the important odd card is between the other two." With the right hand (thumb on the faces, fingers underneath at the bottom) lift these cards off the deck. You appear to hold a fan of only three cards, but you have an unsuspected fourth card behind the last Ace.

Turn the fan face down and place it on the deck. Square the deck and then deal off three cards, face down, in a row. Don't do this quickly; fast motions are suspicious. If you do it slowly everyone should be convinced that the odd card, the Queen, is in the center between the two Aces. Actually, the situation is quite different: You have an Ace between two Queens.

"Now we'll find out if you are awake enough to see what is happening right under your nose. I'll move these cards around a bit — all in slow motion. You try to follow the odd card." Don't call it the Queen. Always refer to it as the *odd* card; you'll see why in a moment.

Slowly transfer the center card to the left end of the row. Then slide the card now in the center to the right, and put the right-hand card in the middle.

The Queen is now, apparently, on the left. *"Can you tell*

figure 30

me where the odd card is now? Just point to it." The spectator indicates the card on your left.

"I suspected that you weren't really very wide awake." Turn the card up, showing it to be an Ace. Then turn up the card in the center, showing the Queen. This is surprise number one. (Don't show the third card yet.)

Turn the Ace and Queen face down again. *"Perhaps that was too complicated. I don't want you to fail this test completely, so I'll make it easier."* This time, merely transpose the left and center cards.

"I hope you followed that. Where is the odd card now?" The spectator again points to the card on your left.

"Now I know you are sound asleep." Turn up the center card, showing the Ace. *"This is the odd card."* The spectators

now think you are the one who is confused. Pause a moment.

"The card you chose can't be the odd card . . ." Turn up the left-hand card, showing the Queen. *". . . because it is like this one."* Turn up the third card, showing another Queen! This final unexpected transformation of an Ace to a Queen is, since everything was done in such slow motion, an eye-popper.

Note that the spectator can't possibly cross you up by not choosing the card you want him to select. If he chooses a Queen the first time, simply end the trick there, showing that it is not the odd card.

7

EASY SLEIGHT OF HAND WITH CARDS

The basic plot of many card tricks is a simple one. A chosen card is buried in the deck and the magician, who seems to have no clue as to its name or location, manages, apparently by some extrasensory perception, to find it.

The magician sometimes does this by providing himself with a secret clue — a *key* or *locator card*. Here is the method in its simplest form.

1. Secretly get a look at, and remember, the bottom card of the deck. This is your key card.

2. Ask a spectator to cut the deck into two heaps, look at the top card of the lower heap, place it on the upper heap, and then complete the cut. This buries the chosen card in the deck and also places the key card directly on the chosen card.

3. If you now spread the deck, you can run your finger back and forth over the cards and display your mystic psychic powers by stopping at the selected card. Merely look for your key card and touch the first card on its right.

It is best, however, to add a pinch or two of psychological misdirection so that any alert spectator who might try to solve the mystery is stopped before he begins. Here's how.

Always make sure that no one sees you taking a look at the bottom card. Here are three ways to get a glimpse of the card in a natural, unsuspicious manner.

1. Hand the deck out to be shuffled and then keep an eye on it. Many people shuffle in a manner that exposes the bottom card. If this fails, use one of the following methods.

2. When you take the deck again, grasp it with your right hand, thumb on the bottom of the deck, fingers on top. As you bring the deck back and place it in the left hand, tilt it just enough to give you a quick glimpse of the bottom card. If you do this in a casual manner, it will pass unnoticed. The spectators aren't really watching you carefully at this point because the trick hasn't really begun.

3. You can also wait until the deck is in your left hand, then turn it into a vertical position and tap the lower end of the cards against the table to square them up. A quick glance downward as you do this tells you the name of the bottom card because it faces you (fig. 31).

Now, just to make absolutely sure that everyone is quite convinced that you can't possibly know the location of any card in the deck, you should shuffle the cards. You use what appears to be a perfectly legitimate shuffle. Actually, it is not quite perfect and, although the other cards are fairly mixed, the key card never leaves the bottom. You can use either the *dovetail* or *riffle* shuffle, which most card players use, or an *overhand* shuffle. You should be able to do either because some card tricks require one, some the other.

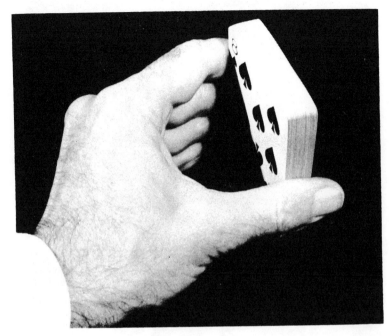

figure 31

riffle shuffle in the air

Most card players shuffle by cutting the deck into two halves
and riffling them together while the cards are on the table.
Many card tricks are performed while you are standing and
you should be able to riffle shuffle the deck without resting
the cards on a table. If you can't do this, here's how.

Take the deck in your right hand, thumb at the inner end,
fingers at the outer end — except for the forefinger which is
curled inward and rests on the top of the deck. Release about
half the cards with the thumb, letting their ends fall onto
the fingers of your left hand. Then place the left forefinger
between the two halves (fig. 32A).

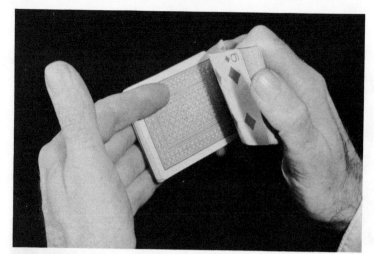

figure 32

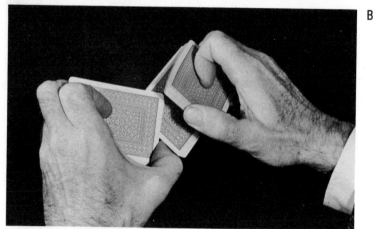

Tilt the lower packet up so that your left thumb can take the opposite edge. Each hand now holds its packet in the same way. Riffle the ends of the cards, interlacing them as in fig. 32**B**. Then push them together. Fig. 32**C** is a view from below showing how the other fingers grip the ends of the cards during the shuffle.

false riffle shuffle

Cut the deck into two halves, hold one half in each hand, and riffle the ends of the cards off your thumbs, letting the cards interweave as they fall. Your left hand, which holds the lower portion of the deck, begins riffling before the right hand starts. This allows a few of the bottom cards to fall first, and the key card on the bottom remains on the bottom.

Notice, too, that if the right hand does not let the top few cards fall until after all those in your hand have been released, the top card of the deck also never changes its position. This, as you will see later, can also be useful.

the overhand shuffle

In a legitimate overhand shuffle, the deck is first held in the usual dealing position. Then the right hand comes under the deck and grasps it at the ends, thumb at the inner end, fingers at the outer end. The right hand lifts the deck up, and the left thumb, pressing against the top of the deck, retains one or more cards in the left hand. The right hand moves down again, and the left thumb draws off a few more cards. This up-and-down action is continued until the left thumb has drawn all the cards off into the left hand.

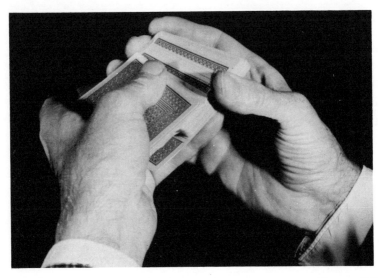

figure 33

false overhand shuffle

Here are two ways to retain control of the bottom card during an overhand shuffle.

1. Shuffle until only three or four cards remain in your right hand. Your left thumb then draws cards down one at a time. The last card to fall, your key card, is now on top of the deck. Now shuffle again and draw down one card only in the first movement of the shuffle. This sends the top card back to the bottom.

2. In the first movement of the shuffle, as your left thumb draws down one or more of the top cards, your left fingers, under the deck, also press against and draw down the bottom card (fig. 33). Shuffle off the remainder of the deck. The original bottom card is still at the bottom.

Both of these shuffles are thoroughly convincing because you really have shuffled all the cards — except for the one important key card.

As added misdirection, keep your eyes off the deck. If you watch the shuffle the audience will do the same and you will be directing their attention to the wrong place at the wrong time.

false cuts

As a final proof that the cards are thoroughly shuffled and that you can't possibly know the location of any of them, follow your shuffle with a cut that looks like the real thing but isn't.

1. Lift off about one-third of the deck and place it on the table. Lift off another third and put it three or four inches to the right. Drop the remaining third between the first two piles. Reassemble the deck by putting the left-hand pile on the center pile, and then the right-hand pile on top of both. Do this carelessly and quickly. It looks fair enough, but the bottom card is still on the bottom.

When you do several card tricks in sequence don't always use the same false cut. Some eagle-eyed spectator might spot it as a phony if he sees it too often. To fool him, do it differently the next time. Here's another method.

2. Cut off the top two-thirds of the deck and place it beneath the cards remaining in your left hand. As you square the deck, insert the flesh at the tip of your left little finger between two portions of the deck — holding a break (fig.34). Now cut off all the cards above the break and drop them on

figure 34

the table. Cut off half the remaining cards and drop them on the first pile; then follow with the rest. The bottom key card is still at the bottom.

Now let's take the methods for discovering a card outlined at the beginning of this chapter and use it as a basis for several tricks. Note how the shuffling and cutting helps conceal the methods used.

the divining knife

A table knife, apparently acting on its own volition, locates a chosen card.

After a spectator has shuffled the deck, glimpse the bottom card using one of the three foregoing methods.

Then shuffle the deck yourself, retaining the key card on the bottom by using one of the false shuffles.

Finally, cut the deck, using one of the false cuts, so that the bottom key card remains on the bottom.

Then have a spectator cut the deck in two heaps, look at the top card of the lower heap, place it on the other heap, and complete the cut. This buries his card somewhere in the center of the deck. Allow the spectator to cut again and then again. This seems to make it impossible for you to know even the chosen card's approximate location. As long as the spectator makes single cuts, his chosen card and your key card will remain together.

Spread the cards in a row, face up. You could finish by simply running your finger back and forth over the cards, and asking the spectator to think *Stop* when your finger is above his card. You apparently read his mind by stopping on the first card to the *right* of the key card.

Here's a better climax with more mystery. Take a table knife (or a long pencil), hold it touching the spectator's forehead, and ask him to think of the name of his card. Then

balance the knife on the side of your forefinger. Pass it slowly along above the cards. When you come to the chosen card,
the knife point swings mysteriously downward and points
to the chosen card (fig. 35). You can pretend that this is a
demonstration of psychomagnetism.

The knife moves because a very slight, imperceptible, forward twist of your forefinger disturbs its balance.

Presented in this manner the trick will fool even those
people who may be aware that a knowledge of the bottom
card is sometimes useful.

Having learned this trick, you will find that you are immediately able to perform the next two tricks. They use
exactly the same means for finding the chosen card, but, because each trick has a different climax, the spectators will
believe them to be different tricks.

figure 35

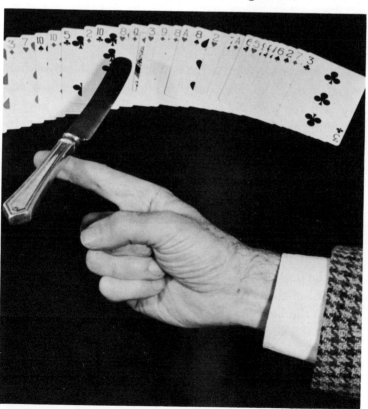

premonition

A psychic hunch from the spirit world locates a chosen card.

Secretly glimpse the bottom card of the deck. Shuffle and cut the deck, retaining this known card on the bottom.

Again, a card is selected and buried in the deck. This can be done just as explained in the preceding trick, but there are other ways of putting the key card next to the chosen card. You should vary this procedure now and then so that the spectators conclude that the manner in which the card is selected and returned to the deck is unimportant. They are wrong, of course, which is exactly what you want.

This time, run the cards from hand to hand and allow the spectator to take any one he likes. After he has looked at it, begin shuffling the cards, using the false overhand shuffle. Say, *"Return your card whenever you like."* As his card comes forward, stop the shuffle and let him replace it on the packet of cards in your left hand.

Your known key card is the bottom card of those you hold in your right hand. Drop all these cards on the chosen one. This puts the key card just above the chosen one.

Another method, even more convincing, is this one. Instead of dropping all the remaining cards onto the chosen cards at once, continue shuffling and, as your left thumb pulls down the next few cards, your left fingers, under the deck, also draw down the bottom card (fig. 33, page 98). Then shuffle off the rest of the cards. This makes it appear that the chosen card must be thoroughly lost among the others.

The chosen card will now, in most cases, be near the center of the deck. Bring it closer to the top by cutting off about one-third of the cards from the top of the deck and placing them on the bottom. This is done so that the dealing of the cards in the next step of the trick won't be too prolonged.

Now for the climax. Begin dealing the cards, one at a time

and place them, face up, in an overlapping row. Tell the spectator, "*When you see the card tell me to stop — not out loud; just think it.*" You can, of course, stop on his card since the known key card immediately precedes it. But here is still a more dramatic, more mysterious way to finish.

When your key card appears, stop the deal. "*Wait! I've just had a psychic message from the spirit world. It says that the next card I turn over will be yours. Name your card, please.*" The spectator names his card, you turn over the next card — and that's it.

booby trap

The performer offers to repeat the **Premonition** trick. This time something seems to go wrong; the spectators believe the magician has made a mistake and are just about to tell him so gleefully, when they find that they have been led into a trap.

Proceed as in **Premonition** until the deal. This time don't stop at the key card or the chosen card. Go right past and deal off half a dozen more cards. Then stop and again announce that you have a premonition. "*The next card I turn over will be yours.*" Push the top card of the deck to the right as though you intended to deal it next (fig. 36, page 104).

Then, before some kind soul can exclaim that you've already passed it, add, "*My hunches are never wrong. In fact, I'll bet any amount of money that the next card I turn over will be the right one.*"

Your boasting, self-confident attitude will help convince the spectators that you are about to fail miserably. Someone may even want to make a bet that you're wrong. You can't lose, of course. Instead of turning over the next face-down card on the deck, reach out and turn the chosen card on the table face down!

figure 36

the magic spell

A spectator finds his own card by spelling to it.

Secretly note the bottom card of the deck, then shuffle, keeping the remembered card on the bottom. Give the deck to a spectator and say, *"Deal as many cards as you like from the top of the deck into a single pile. Stop whenever you get tired. Now, look at the last card you dealt, remember it, and replace it on the pile you dealt. Drop the rest of the deck on top of this pile, then cut the deck.*" He may cut several times. The key card is now next to the chosen card and cutting, provided single cuts are used, will not separate them.

Take the deck again and ask the spectator to concentrate on the name of his card. "*If you concentrate hard enough perhaps I can find it.*" Turn the deck face up and run through it until you find your key card. The chosen card will be the first one to the right of the key card. Note the chosen card's name and then begin spelling it. Begin the spell on the chosen card and push one card to the right for each letter of the name.

For example, if the card was the Five of Clubs, spell: *F-I-V-E O-F C-L-U-B-S*. Then note the name of the next card. Suppose it to be the King of Hearts. Begin with that card and spell *K-I-N-G O-F H-E-A-R-T-S*.

Separate the cards into two groups at this point, gesture toward the spectator with the cards in the right hand, and say, "*You aren't trying. I'm getting nothing but static.*" As your right hand comes back, put the cards it holds *under* those in your left hand. What you have done is to cut the deck, but if you do it as described, it won't be noticed.

Turn the deck face down again. "*Some people just don't broadcast very well.*" Always blame the spectator. "*Maybe you haven't studied that in school yet. Have they taught you to spell? They have? Good. Sometimes you can find a card just by spelling it. Let's take any card as an example. The King of Hearts, for instance.*" (Here you name the *second* card you spelled when you were getting set.)

"*You spell it and I'll deal.*" Deal one card off the deck for each letter. And when the S is reached say, "*If this magic spell is working, this should be the King of Hearts.*" (Name the second card) Show that it is.

"Now you try your card. You take the deck and deal just as I did. If you are a good speller, it should work."

The child, if he can spell, finds his chosen card on the last letter. *"Aren't you glad they teach spelling in school? It comes in very handy."*

a curious prediction

The magician claims to be able to foretell future events and he writes a prediction which comes true.

Ask that the deck be shuffled by a spectator. Insist that it be done thoroughly, and make a point of this so that it will be remembered.

Take the deck after the shuffle and secretly sight the bottom card.

Deal twelve cards in a row face down and ask a spectator to turn any four face up. While this is being done, write the name of the bottom card on a slip of paper, fold it, and give it to someone to hold.

When four of the cards have been turned face up, gather the remaining eight, place them on the bottom of the deck, and then give the deck to a spectator.

Ask him to deal off onto each of the face-up cards enough more face-down cards to bring the total to ten. If there is a seven spot showing he deals three cards onto it. He would deal eight cards onto a two spot, and so on. No additional cards are dealt onto court cards (King, Queen, Jack) because these already have a value of ten.

Finally, have the spectator add the values of the four face-up cards which were chosen at random. A King, three, six and eight, for example, would total twenty-seven. The spectator then deals this number of cards into a separate pile, and turns the last card dealt face up.

The prediction is opened and found to name this last card.

This trick is even more baffling when repeated because the first four cards are different each time.

A word of warning: This works only with a full deck of fifty-two cards.

three tricks in one

You can add three tricks to your repertoire all at once by learning this one. It has three different endings.

First, secretly glimpse the bottom card of the deck, then bring it to the top with an overhand shuffle. Ask a spectator to call out a number and then deal off that many cards, one at a time. This puts the known card at the bottom of the dealt-off heap. Take the top card of the deck and use it to scoop up the dealt cards, so that the known card becomes the second from the bottom.

Give this packet of cards to the spectator. *"You count them, too. Never trust a magician."* See that he counts them in the same way, one at a time. This again reverses their order and puts the known card second from the top.

Turn your back and give these instructions. *"Slide out the bottom card and put it in the center. Do the same with the top card. Turn the next card face up, remember it, show it to everyone, push it in among the others, and then shuffle."*

Although this procedure seems fair enough to the spectator, the card he notes is the one you know, and you merely need to disclose it as effectively as possible.

1. While your back is still turned, add this instruction, *"Don't under any circumstances forget the name of the card; keep repeating it to yourself: Six of Clubs, Six of Clubs, Six of Clubs."* This sudden, unexpected naming of the card he has in mind jolts him and seems to suggest that you have eyes in the back of your head.

2. On another occasion, do the same trick but change the

climax. After the spectator looks at the card, tell him to place it in his pocket. Face him and ask which pocket the card is in. *"I'll use my X-ray vision."* Look closely at the pocket, shake your head, and say, *"All I can see is the back design. Please turn the card face out in your pocket so that I have half a chance."* You don't really need X-ray vision to see this because spectators always put cards in their pockets in this way.

After he has turned the card, look at the pocket again, and pretend that you can see the card. Name the color first, then the suit, and finally the value.

3.   After the card is in the spectator's pocket, gather up all the other cards and reassemble the deck. *"The simplest way to discover the identity of the card in your pocket is to look at all the remaining cards in the deck and find out which one is missing. The trick is to do it fast — like this."*

Face the deck toward yourself, riffle the cards very quickly with your thumb as you watch the faces. Then name the missing card. *"It's easy,"* you add. *"Of course, I had to practice ten hours a day for thirty years."*

the lie detector 1

The performer demonstrates that he can always detect a lie, even while blindfolded.

Once again, your secret weapon is an unsuspected peek at the bottom card of the deck after it has been shuffled. Cut off about two-thirds of the deck and discard it. Give the remaining cards to a spectator, saying *"Please cut this packet into two piles, then look at the top card of either pile, remember it, and replace it on either pile."*

The freedom of choice you allow here is what convinces him that you have no way of finding his card. But since you already know the name of the bottom card of one pile, you are way ahead of him.

If he replaces his card on the pile whose bottom card you know, ask him to cut that pile, burying his card, then place the other pile on top. This puts the card you know next to his.

If he replaces his card on the other pile, simply ask that the remaining pile be replaced on it. Either way, your card and his come together.

Take the packet and say, *"I'll cut the cards several times so that none of us can possibly know where it is."* After the last cut, glance at the bottom card. It it should, by chance, be your key card, cut once more so that the chosen card, now on top, will be buried and won't be the first one dealt.

"Some people's faces give them away when they tell a fib, but I'll do this the hard way — without looking." Blindfold yourself with a handkerchief. Tell the spectator that you will show him the cards one at a time, and ask him to name each one aloud. When his card appears, he is to lie and name some other card. *"Let's see if you can get away with it."*

Warning: Don't let the spectator deal the cards. Since you are blindfolded, he might double-cross you by removing his card and hiding it.

When the spectator calls the name of your key card, you know that the next card is the one he will lie about. As soon as he calls it, whip off your blindfold, point an accusing finger at him, and say, *"That's a lie!"*

the lie detector 2

Children, perhaps because they think they are more experienced prevaricators, often want to match wits with you in "lie detecting" and ask that you do it with them. It is usually best not to repeat the same trick immediately. The first time, the spectators don't know just what is coming and don't know what sort of trickery to watch for, but they have a better chance the second time. You can get around this by repeating what seems to be the same trick if you change the method a bit, as follows.

This time you get a look at and remember the names of the *two* cards that lie at the bottom of the deck. The simplest way is to run through the deck, and look for the Joker, saying that this card is a troublemaker. Note the bottom two cards as you do this and also remember their order. Then give the deck a riffle shuffle, letting several of the bottom cards fall first so that the two you have noted remain on the bottom.

Discard the top two-thirds of the deck and give the remainder to a spectator. Ask him to deal these cards out into two piles. *"This time I will try to detect two liars at once."*

Watch to see on which pile the last card falls. This is the card that was on the bottom of the deck, and the one that was second from the bottom is now the top card of the other pile.

Give these piles to two spectators and ask each one to look at the top card, then shuffle it in among the others. Since you know the names of both cards, detecting lies told about them is a cinch.

Show the cards in the first pile one at a time, and ask the question, *"Is this your card?"* The first spectator is to reply *No* each time a card is shown. When you reach his card you tell him that he is lying.

Pick up the second pile of cards, take a look at the faces and, if necessary, cut the packet so that the chosen card will be among the last to be dealt. Tell the second person he may reply either *Yes* or *No* and may lie about as many cards as he likes. Each time he says *Yes* to a wrong card, tell him he is fibbing. If he lies about his own card, catch him on that, too.

Under these conditions, he may try to cross you up by telling the truth when he sees his own card. If he does, simply say, *"Well, for once I believe you."*

the acrobatic cards

The performer commands a card in the center of the deck to turn face up, and it obeys. Then a card chosen by a spectator also turns face up — at the spectator's command.

Spread a shuffled deck of cards face down on a table and ask a spectator to remove one card. When he has done this, pick up the rest of the cards. *"I'll turn my back while you look at your card and show it to the others."*

While your back is turned, secretly turn the bottom card of the deck face up, note what it is, and leave it face up on the bottom.

Face the spectators again. Hold the deck in your right hand and begin to shuffle the cards overhand into your left hand. Ask the spectator to call *Stop.* When he does so, have him replace his card on those in your left hand. Then drop all the remaining cards on top and square the deck. The reversed card is now just above the chosen card.

"I have spent years training these cards to obey orders. They are so well educated that they even obey impossible orders. For example, if I command the —— of —— (name the face-up card) to flip over so that it is face up in the deck, it will obey instantly. Watch!" Snap your fingers. *"Notice how fast it flipped over? You couldn't see a thing!"*

Spread the cards, and show that the card named is face up. Cut off all the cards above the face-up card and place them on the bottom of the deck. Remove the face-up card with your right hand and hold it up, facing the spectators. *"You did that very well. Take a bow, please."*

While the attention of the spectators is on the "acrobat" card, your left thumb pushes the card now on top of the deck about a half-inch to the right, so that its right edge projects over and covers the left finger tips. Now replace the "acrobat" card, still face up, on this projecting card.

Cover the deck with the right hand, fingers at the outer edge, thumb at the inner edge, and square the deck in the usual manner, except that the left finger tips push up a bit and keep the top two cards slightly separated from the deck.

As soon as both cards are lined up together, lift them off the deck with the right hand as though they were one card (fig. 37).

Immediately turn the deck over with the left hand and place it face up on the apparently single card. Then cut the deck once. This leaves the spectator's chosen card face up in the center of the deck.

Tell the spectator, *"I wonder if your card will obey orders like that? Since I don't know what it is, you will have to do this by yourself."* Place the deck in his left hand. *"Name your card and order it to turn over when you snap your fingers."*

Don't touch the deck again. Have the spectator spread the cards himself. He finds that his card has mysteriously obeyed his command!

figure 37

the magic knife

The performer pushes a table knife into the side of a shuffled deck at the precise spot where a spectator's selected card lies.

Run the cards of a shuffled deck from your left to right hand, and ask a spectator to touch one. *"We won't even take it out of the deck; just touch one."*

When he has done this, spread the cards at this point, and tip them up to show the spectator the face of the card he touched. As he notes it, press your left thumb, behind the cards, against the corner of the touched card, and bend it slightly upward (fig. 38A).

Then push the cards together, square the deck and immediately hand it to someone to shuffle. When you take the deck again, glance at its end and note the position of the card with the bent corner. If it is not visible, turn the deck end for end. If the bent card is close to the top or bottom of the deck, cut the deck to bring it nearer the center.

Place the flat side of the blade of a table knife against the spectator's forehead for a moment, and ask him to think of his card. *"This,"* you explain, *"charges the knife with thought waves."* Rub the knife briskly against your coat sleeve. *"This adds a charge of static electricity. That should do the trick."*

Push the knife into the deck diagonally, inserting it just below the telltale bent corner. Push the knife all the way in, and place your forefinger on the top of the deck. Then dramatically turn the upper portion of the deck over, showing that you have found the selected card. The knife covers and hides the bent corner.

If you are working in a good light, you can add further mystification. After inserting the knife, press it downward against the corner of the deck. This opens the deck slightly, and you can see a reflection of the corner index of the card in the knife blade (fig. 38**B**). Ask the spectator if his card was the ____ of ____ (naming it), and then add, "*I thought so,*" as you turn the upper portion of the deck over, showing the card. The fact that you named the card in addition to finding it with the knife doubles the mystery.

world's record

A spectator chooses a card and shuffles it into the deck himself. The magician places the deck out of sight in his own pocket, and then finds the card in less than three seconds — and with one hand!

This is another use of the bent corner described above. You use the same method but the plot is changed so that, from the audience point of view, it is a quite different trick.

Have a card chosen as in the preceding trick. As the spectators look at its face, bend its corner slightly behind the fan of cards, and let someone shuffle the deck.

Take the deck again and say, "*It's a strange thing which I*

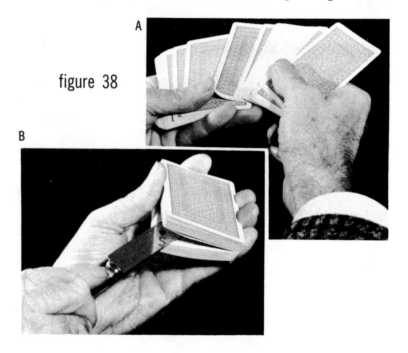

figure 38

can't explain myself, but when I feel lucky I can cut a deck of cards just once and cut directly to any card that is being thought of. Let's try it."

Carefully cut off all the cards that lie above the card with the bent corner. Turn this packet over, exposing the bottom card, scowl at it and say, *"Either this is not my lucky day or you people just aren't concentrating."* Replace the packet underneath the cards in your left hand.

Lift the next card from the deck, turn it so that only you can see it, and take this opportunity to straighten the corner. Scowl again and put it back on the deck, saying, *"No, I missed it completely."*

This is, of course, the chosen card, so remember it.

Again cut off some cards, show the face card, and say, *"Wrong again!"* Since you now know the name of the chosen card you can, if the exposed card is the same color, add, *"It's the right color but everything else is wrong."* If it is not the same color you can say disgustedly, *"It's not even the same color. This is bad."*

Give the cards a riffle shuffle, keeping the top card on top. *"Since I am so unlucky today, there's only one thing I can do to save my reputation as the world's second greatest magician. I'll pass a miracle."*

Put the deck in your jacket pocket. *"I shall now attempt to beat the world's record and find your card while the deck is out of sight using only one hand and — in less than three seconds!"*

Ask the spectators to count to three at the word "Go!" Then go into your pocket quickly and bring out the top card, face down. Ask that the chosen card be named, and then turn up the card you hold very slowly as if you were afraid of more bad luck. Then grin and show that you have finally succeeded.

the magic transformation

Card tricks for younger children should be simple and direct. Their favorite is the sudden, magical transformation of one card into another.

Secretly bend the right inner corner of the bottom card of the deck slightly downward.

Begin the trick by cutting the deck into three piles. Then ask someone to look at the top card of any pile, and replace it on any pile. If the card is replaced on the pile which has the bent card at its bottom, pick that pile up and cut it, then sandwich it between the other two piles. (This puts the bent key card directly above the chosen card.)

If the card is placed on either of the other two piles, simply pick up the pile containing the bent card, drop it on the chosen card, and put both piles on the remaining one. (This gives the same result.)

Square the deck, cut just below the bent card, and then put it and all the cards above it on the bottom of the deck. (This brings the chosen card to the top.)

Give the deck a riffle shuffle, letting the top card fall last so that it stays on top.

Take this top card off the deck with your right hand, turn it to face yourself, and say, "*Your card was not the ——— of ———, was it?*" Don't name the card that faces you; call it anything else. As you do this, push the next card on the deck to the right so that it projects slightly.

When the spectator agrees that the card you named is not his, put it back on the deck. Since the second card projects a bit at the side, it is a simple matter to square the deck and retain the tip of the little finger under the second card at the inner right corner (fig. 39A).

Announce that you will make the chosen card jump to the top of the deck simply by snapping your fingers. Snap your fingers, then grasp the top two cards from above, thumb at the inner edge, fingers at the outer edge — and lift both cards off the deck as one (fig. 39**B**). Press against the ends of the cards, bending them slightly. (This insures that they will remain together.)

figure 39

A

B

Show the face of the card to the audience. *"There, you see how easy it is."* Immediately replace the card(s) on the deck.

When the spectators tell you that the card shown is not the correct one, look surprised, lift off the top card (one only this time), glance at it yourself, and lay it aside, face down. *"That's odd, first time I ever missed. I'll try again."*

Cut off a group of cards, turn them face up, and show the card on the bottom. *"Then this must be your card."* They deny this, too.

Replace these cards, cut at another spot, and show another wrong card. By now the small fry, all little sadists at heart, are enjoying your failure. *"I think you're pulling my leg. Just what card are you thinking of?"*

When they name it, point at the face-down card you laid aside and object, *"But that was the first card I showed you!"*

Don't turn it up yourself; wait and let them grab for it.

Children always want to see this again so get set for it before they ask. Just as someone turns the face-down card over and everyone's attention is concentrated there, bring your hands together, push the top card of the deck over to one side, and flip it over, face up, on the deck. Square it with the rest of the cards and again insert the flesh at the tip of your little finger under the corner of the card. Keep the deck turned inward so that the reversed card can't be seen.

Retrieve the chosen card, put it face up on the reversed card, square the deck and turn it so that the top card can be seen. *"What card did you think this was?"* As they answer, grasp both cards along the right side edge between forefinger and thumb and turn them face down as one card. Then, immediately take off the top card with your right hand.

Ask a child to blow on it, then turn it over slowly, showing that it has mysteriously changed back again!

mathematical discovery

Another card is chosen and then discovered in a nonsensical manner.

The bent-corner key card is on the bottom at the start. A card is chosen, and returned so that it is below the locator as in the preceding trick. It's the same method, but the story and the climax are quite different.

"*Sometimes you don't need magic to find a card; you can do it by mathematics. Like this. You cut the deck three times.*" Do this as you talk, the last time cutting just below the bent card so that the chosen card is brought to the top.

"*Then take the card on top . . .*" Lift this off, look at it yourself but don't show it. "*. . . multiply it by forty-two, add sixteen, take the square root, and subtract the age of the person who chose the card. How old are you?*"

When the spectator gives his age, scratch your head and say slowly, "*When I subtract that — my answer is the —— of ——.*" (Name the card you hold.)

Pause a moment, then add, "*Of course it takes an awful lot of practice to be able to do all those mathematics in your head.*" On the last word, lay down the card you hold, face up. When they see that *this* is the chosen card, you get a laugh because it completely exposes your boast that you are a lightning calculator.

the power of thought

A chosen card appears at a number selected by the spectator.

Your bent-corner key card is on the bottom at the start. Any card is chosen and returned to the deck, the locator going on top of it. Cut at the locator, bringing the chosen card to the top, and then riffle shuffle, retaining it there.

Tell the spectator to call out any number between one and twenty, and add, *"If you think of that number hard enough your card will appear there."*

Suppose he calls "eight." Deal eight cards onto the table, one at a time. Turn up the last card dealt. *"Is this your card? No? Then you aren't thinking hard enough."*

Put the dealt cards back on the deck. (Because the order of the cards was reversed during the deal, the chosen card is now the eighth card from the top.) Before you count again, cut the deck once, then again, this time at the locator card.

Say, *"Try again. Think harder this time."* Deal the same number of cards as before. Before you turn up the last card, ask that the chosen card be named. Then show it.

double trouble

The magician tries to outdo himself by finding two chosen cards simultaneously in world-record time. He succeeds in finding one card only, but extricates himself from this predicament by causing the first card to change magically into the second one.

Use two spectators who are not sitting near each other. We'll call the first one John. Give him the deck to be shuffled, then ask him to call out any number between one and twenty. (You limit him to this so that the necessary dealing is not too protracted.)

Tell him to deal that many cards off the deck, one at a time. When he has done this, take the remainder of the deck and turn your back. Ask John to look at the last card he dealt without letting anyone else see it. While he is doing this, bend the lower right-hand corner of the bottom card downward slightly.

Face John again, drop the deck on his pile of cards. Square the deck and cut it. Then cut a second time just below the locator card which brings it to the bottom and John's card to the top.

Go to a second spectator, Mary, let us say. Ask her also to call a number. This time deal that many cards yourself rather fast. Then tell her, *"Just to make sure I did that right, you count them too."* See that she counts them in the same way, dealing them one at a time. *"Now look at the top card."* She sees the *same* card that John chose.

Replace the rest of the deck on top of her pile, and again cut below the locator, bringing the chosen card to the top. Riffle shuffle, retaining it there.

Now build up the feat you are about to do. *"I am going to find both cards simultaneously in less than two seconds — a new world's record! And I'll do it with one hand, with both eyes closed, and while the deck is in my pocket!"*

Put the cards in your pocket, roll up your sleeve, and close your eyes. *"Ready! Get set! Go!"* Plunge your hand into your pocket, grab the top card, and bring it out as fast as you can. Keep the card face down, scowl at it, and say, *"That's funny! I only got one card. It's the first time that ever happened."*

Go to John and show him the card, but hold it so that Mary can't see it. *"Is this your card?"* He says it is. *"Well, at least the one I did get was right."*

Go to Mary. *"I'm sorry I didn't get your card. Let's try something else. It might work. Think of your card just as hard as you can and make a magic pass over this one."* Then look at the face of the card and shake your head. *"No. You didn't think hard enough. Try it again!"* Glance at the card again. *"That's better! Is this it?"* Show it to her without letting John see it. She agrees that that card is hers. Thank her for her expert assistance, return the card to the deck, and proceed with something else.

Most of the spectators will believe the card really did change because it seems so unlikely that both people could have chosen the same card. Even if John or Mary compare notes out loud and everyone realizes that the card didn't actually change, they are still left with the mystery of how two people both happened to choose the same card.

detective story

A card chosen by a spectator plays the part of a criminal. It escapes into the underworld (the rest of the deck) and is lost by shuffling. The four Kings, playing the parts of law-enforcement officers, are placed in the center of the deck and mysteriously manage to find the wanted man.

Run the cards across from your left to right hand and ask a spectator to touch one. Lift the card he touches, together with all the cards above it, into a vertical position so that he can see the face of the card he chose. *"That card is Public Enemy Number One, a notorious bank robber. Remember his name. You are a witness."*

The fingers of your left hand square up the cards they hold and the little finger presses tightly against the inner right corner of the packet. Replace the cards in your right hand on those in your left. Square the deck, but continue to press inward with your left little finger, so that a small opening is maintained in the corner of the deck (fig. 40A, page 125).

Cut off all the cards above the opening and put them on the table. Cut off about half the remaining cards, and place them on the first heap. Then, drop the rest of the deck on top. This triple cut looks fair enough, but it has brought the chosen card to the bottom of the deck.

Pick up the deck with your right hand, and, as you place it in your left, tilt it just enough to get a quick glimpse of the chosen card on the bottom. Then cut the deck again immediately.

"*The criminal has made his escape into the underworld and keeps moving around so the police can't find him. You shuffle the underworld so he's completely lost.*" Give the deck to a spectator to shuffle.

Take the deck again, hold it with the faces toward yourself, and run through the cards until you come to a King. Take all the cards above the King and cut them to the back of the deck, leaving the King on the face.

Meanwhile, you are saying, "*Four of these cards — the Kings — are detectives.*" Continue running through the cards and as you come to each King pull it out and put it on the face of the deck. Also watch for the chosen criminal card. When you see it, take it out, just as though it were a King. Since they are not aware that you cut one King to the face of the deck before you started hunting for the Kings, the spectators will assume that the four cards you removed are all Kings.

Spread the top five cards slightly, note the position of the chosen card, then remove the five cards in a bunch. Keep these cards well squared from here on so that no one can see that you have more than four.

Lay the rest of the deck aside. Transfer any Kings that lie behind the chosen card to the face of the packet, so that the chosen card is on the back of the packet.

Now deal off each card singly, showing that you have only four Kings. Like this. Turn your hand so the spectators can see the face card. Your thumb should lie along one edge of the cards, the tips of the other fingers along the opposite edge.

"*This King is the Chief of Police.*" Place your second finger on the King, draw it back toward you, then lift it off, and put it on the table or floor.

Deal the next two Kings off in the same manner, saying,

"This second King is the District Attorney, the third is an FBI man."

Deal the fourth King and the chosen card, which is under it as one card. Simply take them with your first finger at their outer end and your thumb at their inner end, and place them on the cards already dealt. *"This last King is the world's best-known private eye — Sherlock Holmes."*

And now, so that everyone is thoroughly convinced that the situation is as you say, you show each King singly once more, but in a slightly different fashion.

Pick up the cards and hold them face down. Push the top card forward, lift it at the outer end, and turn it end-for-end. Square it with the others and name it again. *"The Chief of Police."* Push it slightly to the right with your thumb and lift it off, taking it at the ends between thumb and second finger. Place it on the table.

Turn the next card over. *"The District Attorney."* Deal it off in the same way.

Turn the third card face up. *"The FBI man."* This time you deal two cards as one. This way. Place your right second finger at the outer right-hand corner, your thumb at the inner right corner. As you begin to move the three cards toward the right, the tips of the left fingers underneath press against the bottom card and hold it back (fig. 40**B**). Your right hand continues moving to the right and carries the top two cards away as one. Place them on the previously dealt Kings.

Turn the last card face up. *"Sherlock Holmes."* Then place it on the others.

The rest is easy. Ask a spectator to cut off about half of the face-down deck. Put the squared-up Kings *face up* on the lower half of the deck. The spectator drops his half on top.

"The four detectives go into the underworld and start their manhunt." Riffle the end of the deck. *"All the underworld characters are nervous. But it doesn't take four great detectives long to round up a suspect. Look!"*

figure 40

A

B

Spread the deck out, showing the four face-up Kings with one face-down card between them. *"They've arrested somebody. Will our witness now please testify as to the wanted criminal's identity?"*

He names the chosen card. Turn up the face-down card. *"The case is solved. They got him!"*

8

PREPARED CARD MIRACLES

Some of the most astonishing effects in card magic are those which utilize the principle of secret prearrangement of the cards. Here are several that can make your reputation as a magician.

the four aces

A spectator deals himself a number of cards as directed by the audience and gets the four Aces.

The advance secret preparation consists in placing the four Aces on top of the deck and then putting eight other cards above them, so that the Aces are the ninth, tenth, eleventh, and twelfth cards down from the top of the face-down deck.

Begin by giving the deck a false riffle shuffle as follows.

Cut off somewhat more than half the cards with your right hand, and riffle shuffle these into the remaining cards held in your left hand. Let the cards fall from the left hand faster than from the right, so that the left-hand packet is exhausted before the top thirteen cards in the right-hand group are reached. Square the deck and repeat the shuffle. If you do this casually and without comment, no one will suspect that the shuffle is not as thorough as it might be.

Ask a spectator to assist you, and tell him that you are going to teach him a new game. *"Most people, for some reason, never trust a magician in a card game so I'll let you do the dealing."*

Give him the deck. *"The dealing rules are unusual. You always let the other players tell you how many cards to deal. Will someone please call a number between ten and twenty?"*

Suppose sixteen is called. Instruct the dealer to deal sixteen cards one at a time, face down, into your hand.

"Another dealing rule states that the digits of the called number must be added together, and that many cards dealt back onto the deck. This makes it impossible for the dealer to cheat. Six and one are seven so I'll deal seven cards back on to the deck." You also deal the cards one at a time.

Take the top card from those in your left hand and lay it out face down. Finally, place the dealt-off pile of cards back on the deck.

Ask someone else to call another number between ten and twenty, and go through the same procedure. Do this four times in all, so that you end with four cards laid out face down.

"Each player," you explain, *"deals four cards in this way and the one who gets the most high cards wins. If we were playing for money you would win ten dollars for each King, Queen, or Jack, and twenty-five dollars for each Ace. Let's see if you were lucky enough to win anything."*

Turn the four face-down cards up slowly, one at a time, disclosing a hundred dollars worth of Aces!

Look at the dealer suspiciously. *"I wonder where a boy (or girl) of your age learned to do that? You go right back and sit down. I am not going to play cards with you. I'd lose my shirt."*

prize contest

The performer announces a prize contest. Three spectators compete and although the odds are greatly against anyone's winning, *everybody* wins.

Your advance preparations consist in placing four Kings together on top of the face-down deck, and then four indifferent cards on top of the Kings. Also bend the inner right corner of the bottom card slightly for a locator.

Announce that you are going to hold a prize contest, and select three contestants.

Riffle shuffle the deck, allowing the bottom card to fall first and the top cards last, so that the eight top cards are not disturbed.

Deal four cards in a row, face up. Then say, *"Sorry, that's not right. I should have dealt those cards face down."* Gather the cards and put them on the bottom of the deck. Deal four more cards, face down this time. These are all Kings but the spectators will assume that they are all different because the four cards you dealt face up, apparently by mistake, were different.

Ask someone to choose one of the four cards and place it in his pocket, without looking at it or letting anyone else see it. *"That card will determine the winner of the contest."*

Put the remaining three cards back on the deck, and cut the deck. Then cut again, this time just below the bent card.

This brings the three Kings back to the top, with four indifferent cards above them.

Now deal four hands of cards, just as you would in dealing four hands of bridge, but deal only six cards to each hand. The first three hands each have a King as the second card from the bottom.

Give one of these hands to each contestant. Take the fourth hand for yourself. "*Now, each of you do just what I do.*" Take your top card and put it on the bottom of your packet. Deal off the next card, and discard it. Continue this operation, dealing one card under and discarding the next — until only one card remains. See that the three spectators all do the same.

Then say, "*This is probably the toughest prize contest in the world. I've been doing this for years and nobody has won anything yet.*" Ask the person who has the chosen card in his pocket to bring it out and show it. Turn to the contestants. "*If any of you has a King, he wins the Grand Prize!*"

All three contestants have Kings! "*That's impossible!*" Pretend not to believe it. You are, of course, prepared for this, and you pay off with three prizes, lollipops, perhaps.

double discovery

Two cards are chosen by two spectators who shuffle them back into the deck themselves. There seems to be no possible way in which the performer could know either the identity or location of the cards, and yet he finds both *simultaneously*.

Your advance preparation consists in dealing the deck into two piles, placing all the odd cards in one pile, and all the even cards in another. (The Jacks and Kings, having values of eleven and thirteen, are odd, the Queens are even.)

Take either pile, hold it face down, and bend the ends upward so that the whole packet is slightly concave. Place the other pile on top of it. The bend in the lower packet leaves a break in the side edge of the deck which marks the center of the pack (fig. 41).

You cannot shuffle this stacked deck as the trick begins, and yet your audience must believe that the cards are well mixed. You convince them of that this way. Place a rubber band around one end of the stacked deck, half an inch from the end, and put it in your coat pocket. Do a trick or two, using another deck (having the same back design) in the course of which the cards are legitimately shuffled. Then pretend you have finished with card tricks and put this deck in the same pocket that holds the stacked deck. Do a trick of a different sort — a coin or rope trick perhaps. Then remember another card trick. Reach into your pocket, push the rubber band off with your thumb and bring out the stacked deck. The exchange is so simple and direct that it is never suspected.

Look for the break in the side of the deck, and cut off all the cards above it. Hold half the deck on the palm of each hand, and ask two spectators to select cards simultaneously, one from each half. *"Cut off any number of cards, take one from the center, and replace the others, but don't look at*

figure 41

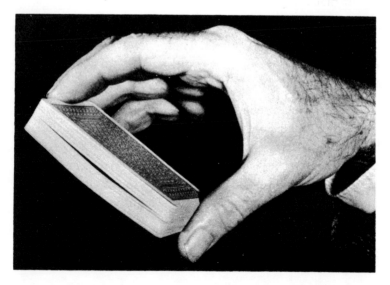

your chosen cards until I have turned my back. We want to be absolutely sure that I don't see either of them."

When you have turned away, bring your hands together, place the right packet in the left hand and vice versa. Face the audience again, and give the right-hand packet to the spectator on your right, the other to the spectator on your left. Tell them to push their chosen cards back in among the others they hold, and then shuffle the cards thoroughly.

Because of your hand-to-hand exchange of packets one person shuffles his odd card among the even ones; the other, his even card among the odd ones. When the shuffling is done, take both packets and place them together.

"Two cards have been chosen while my back was turned. Both have been thoroughly shuffled into the deck. There is no possible way I can find either card — unless you help me by broadcasting thought waves. Please concentrate on your cards."

Turn the deck to face yourself and run through the cards. Look for an even card among odd ones, or the reverse. When you find the first card take it and all the cards above it into your right hand for a moment. Point with this hand toward the first spectator. If it is a boy, say, *"You have girls on your mind. Please, try to forget them for just a moment and think of your card."* If it is a girl, of course, you say she is thinking about boys. Then replace the cards in your right hand under those in your left. This puts the first chosen card on top of the deck.

Turn to the second spectator. *"While he's trying to do that, let's see how you are doing."* Continue to run through the cards until you find the second out-of-place card. Shift it to the face of the deck. Scowl at it dubiously, then shake your head. *"No, that's not it. Most of the thought waves coming from your direction are filled with static. I think you need a new vacuum tube."*

Turn the deck face down and riffle shuffle without disturbing the top or bottom cards. Look back at the first spectator. *"He's got it bad. Girls. Girls. Girls. This puts me in a very embarrassing position. I shall have to use real magic."*

Put the deck in your pocket, go to the first spectator and touch his forehead with one finger. *"That's better — not much — but it helps."* Do the same to the second spectator. *"What a horrible noise! I think you need a complete tune-up job."*

Raise your right hand and pull your sleeve back a bit. *"Well, I'll take a chance."* Go into your pocket, grasp the deck on opposite sides, pull up the top and bottom cards and bring them out together. Ask that the chosen cards be named, then show that you have found them both.

everyone takes a card

Several spectators select cards while the deck is spread face down on the table and the magician is at some distance from it. They replace the cards under the same conditions, anywhere in the deck. Nothing could be fairer. It seems impossible that the magician could find even one card — but he finds them all!

The method is simplicity itself. The whole deck is stacked. All the cards of each suit are together and in numerical order. Do another trick or two first with another deck, and then switch it in your pocket for the stacked deck, as explained on page 130.

You may cut the stacked deck one or more times without disturbing the arrangement of the cards. Do it this way. Hold the deck in your right hand as though you were about to give it an overhand shuffle. Pull about half the cards down into the left hand, then throw the remaining cards on top. This merely cuts the deck. If you do this casually three or four times, the spectators will mistake it for a shuffle.

Spread the cards in a line across the table or on the floor. Step away from them and ask several people to take one card each from anywhere in the spread.

When this has been done, scoop up the cards, square the deck, and spread it out again. Don't forget to do this; it prevents anyone from replacing his card in the same position from which he drew it.

Ask that all the cards be returned *"Anywhere at all."* Then gather the cards again and give them another cut or two. All you have to do now is to look through the cards and find those that are not in their proper sequence. But don't make it look that easy.

Ask the spectators who drew the cards to concentrate on them, pretend to do some heavy concentrating yourself, and accuse one or two people of not thinking hard enough. This is pure, unadulterated misdirection but it dramatizes what you are doing, and makes it appear difficult, and gets more applause at the finish.

Take out each misplaced card as you find it and put it aside, face down. After you have found the last card, shuffle the deck, destroying the arrangement. Then ask that the chosen cards be named, and show each one as it is called.

mental spell

The discovery by the performer of a card which has been *mentally* selected by a spectator is one of the most mystifying of all card feats. Here the performer accomplishes this miracle twice. You will find that the effect is well worth the small amount of preparation required.

Remove the following cards from the deck, and arrange them in two groups as listed below. The order given is from top to bottom with the cards face down.

1	2
Jack of Clubs	Two of Spades
Four of Hearts	Queen of Clubs
Queen of Spades	Ten of Diamonds
Five of Diamonds	King of Diamonds
Eight of Diamonds	Seven of Diamonds

Put either group on the other and place them both on top of the deck. Bend the inner right corner of the bottom card of the deck downward, put ten other cards below it, and the Two of Hearts below those.

It is best not to perform this trick as the first of a series of card tricks for two reasons. The deck cannot be shuffled as you begin because your arrangement would be destroyed, and the effect produced by the trick is so strong that it should be done as a finale. Put a rubber band around the stacked deck, and carry it in your pocket until needed. Do a few other tricks with another deck having the same back design, then switch decks as described under **Double Discovery** on page 129.

Announce that you are going to perform an extremely difficult trick which requires complete silence. Stress this so that the spectators will know they are about to see something extraordinary and will pay close attention. The closer they watch the more impossible it seems.

Take the top five cards off the deck, spread them in a fan, and hold it before a spectator. Turn your head away so that you can't see his face and tell him, *"I want you to select any one of these cards. Don't touch it or take it out. Just mentally choose one and make sure you remember it."*

After he has done this, drop these cards on the table, take the next five cards, and have a second person mentally choose one in the same way. Then put these five cards back on the deck, and replace the first group on them.

Give the deck a complete cut. Then cut again, this time just below the bent card. This puts the Two of Hearts and ten other cards above the two arranged groups.

"One way to find a card that has been lost in the deck is to name it, snap your fingers above the deck, spell the card's name, and then deal one card for each letter. Like this. Suppose I'm hunting for the Two of Hearts . . ."

Spell out *T-W-O O-F H-E-A-R-T-S*, and deal one card face down for each letter. Turn up the card that appears on the letter S and show the Two of Hearts. Get this card out of the way by pushing it into the center of the deck. Pick up the other ten cards and replace them on top of the deck.

Turn to the first person who mentally selected a card. *"Of course, I can't do that with your card because I haven't the vaguest notion what it is. Only you know. So you'll have to perform the magic. Hold your hand above the deck and snap your fingers. That's fine! It wasn't hard, was it? Now begin spelling your card one letter at a time."* As he does this, deal one card for each letter. Make sure he spells out the "of."

It doesn't matter which of the five cards he mentally selected. Each card in the first group, reading from the top down, spells out with one more letter than the preceding one. Whatever card he spells must turn up on the final letter.

As you deal, count the first five cards into a neat pile, and then deal the sixth card a bit off center so that it projects beyond the others. Deal the remaining cards so that they line up with the first five.

When the spelling is completed, show that the last card is the one that was mentally selected. Congratulate the spectator. *"You did that very well!"*

Place this selected card on those that were dealt off, and then pick up the projecting sixth card, together with all the cards above it. Put them back on *top* of the deck. Place the remaining five cards on the *bottom* of the deck. This sets things so that the second chosen card will spell out.

Ask the second spectator to snap his fingers and spell out his mentally-selected card as you deal. He also succeeds. Congratulate him and ask both spectators to stand and take a bow.

the great jail escape

Most people believe that the hand is quicker than the eye and are, therefore, suspicious of any quick movement on the magician's part. This trick is a real baffler because it is all done in slow motion. It will give you a reputation as a sleight-of-hand expert, in spite of the fact that no sleight of hand at all is used. Also, its entertainment value for children is first-rate because of the story that goes with it.

You need two Jacks of Spades. Place one in your outer breast pocket. Cut a diagonal section from the other Jack of Spades and place it on the Nine of Diamonds as shown on the right in fig. 42A. Mark the position of the Jack by drawing a light pencil line on the nine along the Jack's left edge. Turn the Jack over to the left, face down, keeping its edge lined up with the pencil line. This position is shown on the left in fig. 42A. Apply a strip of Scotch tape along the edge to serve as a hinge.

Use rubber cement to attach a plain white three-by-five index card onto any other playing card, covering its face. Trim away the excess, and letter the words OUT TO LUNCH on the card with a Magic Marker (fig. 42B). (The Joker may also be used instead of this card.) Put this OUT TO LUNCH card face up on the nine, put the three on both, and carry them in your pocket.

As you begin the trick, bring out these three cards, and hold them with their backs toward the spectators. Spread them in a fan, and slip the OUT TO LUNCH card under the hinged flap. Make sure that the top edges of this card and the Jack line up (fig. 42B). Place the three on both these cards as shown in fig. 42C.

"I'd like to tell you a story about the old West. I was the sheriff of Deadwood Gulch in those days, and one morning the Jack of Spades robbed the stage coach." Show the fan of three cards to your audience.

"I sent two of my deputies after him — the Three of Hearts and the Nine of Diamonds — and they caught him." Grasp the upper right corner of the Jack between thumb and forefinger (fig. 42C) and turn the backs of the cards toward the spectators.

"They brought him into town and put him in the jail." Lift the center card up slowly, and lay it out face down. As you do this, your left thumb slides the three to the left so that it covers the Jack (fig. 42D).

Show the faces of the remaining two cards to the spectators, turn them backs out again, and place the Nine of Diamonds face down to the right of the first card. *"The Nine of Diamonds knew that Jack was a slippery character so he stood guard at the front door."* Show the face of the third card. *"And the Three of Hearts guarded the back door."* Place it face down on the left.

A

B

figure 42

C

D

E

"*Now I'm going to swear you all in as deputies. Have you all been watching? Do you all know where Jack is?*" Everything has been done so slowly and convincingly that the spectators have to agree that Jack is safely in the jail — the card in the middle.

"*Good,*" you say, "*but keep your eyes on him. He wasn't in that jail five minutes before he managed to get out of his cell, slip around to the back door and knock the Three of Hearts on the head.*" Lift the center card and tap it against the back of the card on the left. "*Then he sneaked up on the guard at the front door and knocked him out, too.*" Tap the other card in the same way and then replace the card you hold in the center.

"*When I got down to the jail — I was late for work that morning — I found both guards sound asleep.*" Pick up the two red cards, one in each hand put the three on the nine and show them (fig. 42E).

"*And when I looked in Jack's cell — I found this.*" Show the face of the remaining card. The Jack has vanished and you hold a sign that reads: OUT TO LUNCH.

"*Of course, if all you deputies were watching, you saw where he went. No? Well, we found him a few days later hiding out up in the hills.*" Reach into your outer breast pocket and bring out the Jack.

We repeat: fast movements are both suspicious and confusing, and, in this trick, quite unnecessary.. Do everything slowly and deliberately. This makes all your actions appear to be so fair and above suspicion that the sudden transformation of the Jack and its final reappearance come as real surprises.

One other thing: when you ask if everyone knows where the Jack is, a spectator will sometimes try to cross you up by pretending he believes it to be one of the end cards.

When this happens, simply pick up both of the end cards, put the three on the nine so that it hides the flap, show both, and ask, *"Have you been sound asleep?"* Then replace both cards as they were and continue.

9

HOW TO READ MINDS

color clairvoyance

The performer proves (by magician's logic) that he can distinguish between colors without seeing them.

Display several wax crayons of the sort that children use with coloring books. *"Magic,"* you begin, *"is sometimes very useful. When I'm driving my car I never need to look at a traffic light to know whether it is red, yellow, or green. I just guess — and I'm always right. I'll show you."*

Put your hands behind your back, and turn away from the audience. *"Select one of the crayons and give it to me behind my back."* When this has been done, face the audience again.

Behind your back, dig the nail of the middle finger of your right hand into the end of the crayon and scrape off a small piece of the colored wax. Bring this hand to the front, place it against your forehead, and concentrate. If you keep the fingers curled inward as your hand moves up to your forehead, you can spot the particle of crayon under the fingernail, and note its color.

Don't name the color immediately; that makes it look too easy. Pretend that what you are doing is difficult, and that you really are receiving faint mental impressions. Also, as should be done in most mind-reading tricks, give the information out piecemeal. *"I get the impression of a light color . . . yellow, perhaps, or orange . . . I feel it more clearly now . . . the color is yellow!"* This adds suspense and is dramatically effective.

Finally, prove that the trick wasn't just a lucky guess by doing it again once or twice.

seeing with the finger tips

Several colored objects are given to the magician behind his back and he apparently distinguishes one color from another by touch.

Any small, differently colored objects may be used — crayons, pencils, swizzle sticks, soda straws. In advance, push about four such objects, crayons, let us say, under the band of your wrist watch and up along the inner side of your arm (fig. 43). Memorize the order of the colors from left to right.

figure 43

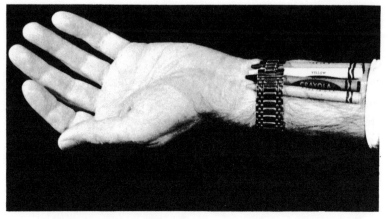

Begin the trick by handing out four duplicates. *"I can,"* you announce, *"tell one color from another by sense of touch alone. I can see color with my finger tips. Mix these colored crayons and then hand them to me behind my back."*

After this has been done, face the audience again. Behind your back place the crayons in your hip pocket. Ask someone to name one of the colors. Immediately pull the crayon of the proper color from the memorized group that you have hidden up your sleeve, and toss it out.

Then produce the remaining colors, as called for. Do this rapidly; the faster it is done, the more difficult it seems to be.

magic arithmetic

A spectator is given a pad and pencil and asked to write down any number of three different figures. Then he is to reverse this number (for example: 673 reversed gives 376) and subtract the smaller number from the larger.

In most problems of this sort the performer, given the final answer, names the original number. But here, apparently knowing nothing at all, he concentrates and gives the answer.

Stand away from the spectator so that you can't see what is written but keep an eye on the movements of the spectator's pencil.

The answer usually contains three figures; occasionally only two. It is easy to tell by watching the pencil when the spectator writes a two-figure answer. You always know immediately what this is because a two-figure answer is *always* 99.

In a three-figure answer, the middle digit is *always* 9, and the two outside digits *always* add up to 9. You have two chances to get the information you need. It is easier than you think to recognize the number being written by watching the pencil. If you get either the first or last number, you know the other number. For example, if 2 is the first number written (in subtracting, the answer is written from right to left) the three-digit answer must be 792.

Don't announce the whole number. Ask the spectator to concentrate first on the first digit of the answer. Do this even though you may have failed to recognize the number from the pencil movements.

Then name the first digit. If necessary, just make a guess. If you are correct, the trick is as good as done because you know what the other two numbers must be. If you have made an error, or are simply guessing and are wrong, accuse the spectator of not concentrating hard enough, and ask for the number.

"Let's take the second digit, and please concentrate on it hard. I can't get any thought waves unless you broadcast a few."

This time you are correct; the second digit is always 9.

Since you now know the first digit, subtracting it from 9 gives you the third digit. Even if you fail on the first digit, your ability to pull the rest of the answer out of thin air is impressive.

After having done this two or three times so that the spectators realize that different answers are obtained, throw in this variation. Any number of three different figures is reversed, and the smaller subtracted from the larger as before. Then the answer is reversed, and this new figure added. *Example*:

$$
\begin{array}{r}
845 \\
-548 \\
\hline
297 \\
+792 \\
\hline
1{,}089
\end{array}
$$

This time you can keep your back turned during the whole

trick, and get every digit of the answer every time. This procedure *always* gives an answer of 1,089.

numbers in the mind

There are several mathematical tricks in which the performer discovers a mentally-selected number after the spectator
has performed some calculations with it and announced his
result. This trick is much more mystifying. The spectator
begins with an unknown number, and the performer gives
the final answer without knowing the original number and
without asking any questions.

Ask someone to think of a number and then pretend to
concentrate. *"Ninety-five thousand, seven hundred and sixty-
two. No! Not such a big number, please. That is much too
difficult. Less than ten, please. Good. That's much better."*
Then tell him to make the following calculations:

> Double the number,
> Add 8,
> Divide by 2,
> Subtract the original number.

*"Now concentrate on your answer. You are thinking . . . of
the number . . . four!"*
This will be correct because the answer is *always* half the
number you told him to add, in this instance, 8. *Example:*
$6 \times 2 = 12 + 8 = 20 \div 2 = 10 - 6 = 4$.

Now, before anyone has time to think about it and realize
that the answer may always come out the same, do it again.
Have a different number added and get a different answer.

At first give even numbers to be added. Then, the last
time, ask the spectator to add an odd number, such as 9. The
final result will now contain a fraction. The spectator, dis-

covering this, is always pleased; he thinks that this will prove too difficult. Let him think that until the last possible moment.

"You are thinking of the figure two . . . but something's wrong! You are also thinking of a one . . . and a four. Please don't try to mislead me like that. The answer can't possibly be two hundred and fourteen. Oh, I see . . . you are thinking — four and one-half."

the z-ray tube

The performer exhibits a paper cylinder which he says enables him to see through solid objects. He uses it to look through a spectator's hand, through a book, and, finally, demonstrates that it works even for the spectators.

The following three tricks may be done separately, but they are much more effective when presented, as here, in a single routine.

Roll a sheet of paper into a tube about eight inches in length and one inch in diameter. Encircle it with a rubber band.

Place three coins of different denominations on the table or floor and cover them with a book.

Select a spectator to assist you, turn your back, and give him the following instructions: *"Lift the book and take out one of the coins. Now decide in which hand you want to hold it, then close your fist tightly on the coin. Place the hand that holds the coin against your forehead and count, aloud, from one to fifteen. Then lower your hand and hold both hands side by side, fists closed."*

When this has been done, face the spectator and call attention to the paper tube. *"This tube,"* you say with a straight face, *"is a Z-ray machine. It does the same work as an X-ray machine, but it's much better because it is less expensive, it's portable, and you don't have to wait to get the pictures developed. I invented it last night."*

Approach the spectator and look through the tube at each of his hands. *"You're holding the coin in that hand."* Point to the correct hand. (You'll find out how in a moment.)

Go to the book, examine it through the tube for a moment. Turn your back again. *"Now, please replace the coin under the book with the others."*

After this has been done, turn, take the book away and push each coin forward slightly with your forefinger. *"Looking through the book with the Z-ray tube I could see that the quarter* (name whichever coin is correct) *wasn't there, so that must be the one you were holding."*

The Z-ray tube, of course, is entirely misdirection. The secret is much simpler than Z rays. As soon as you turn to face the spectator the first time, glance at his hands. Some of the blood will have left the hand he has been holding to his forehead, and it will be paler than the other.

Another Holmesian clue tells you which coin was used. When you remove the book and push each coin forward, they will all feel slightly cold to the touch except one. This one has picked up heat from the spectator's hand, and is the one you name.

Now for the final astonishing proof that Z rays really work as you claim. Give the tube to a spectator and ask him to look through it. Instruct him to keep both eyes open. Place your hand over the opposite end of the tube.

"Are the Z rays penetrating my hand? Can you see through it?" He says, "No."

"That's odd. All my laboratory tests show that Z rays never fail. Oh. I see. You're looking through the wrong end of the tube. Turn it around."

This time, instead of covering the end of the tube with your hand as before, put it close to the side of the tube, three

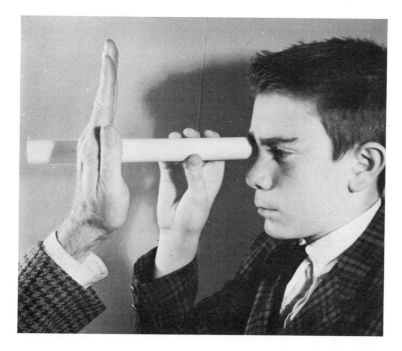

figure 44

or four inches in from the end (fig. 44). The spectator sees a neat round hole drilled right through your hand. The illusion is perfect.

money mind reading

A spectator conceals a nickel in one hand, a dime in the other, and you discover which hand contains which coin.

Tell him to multiply the value of the coin in his right hand by 4, then multiply the value of the coin in the left hand by 7. Ask him to add the two answers and give you the total.

You immediately announce which coin each hand contains. If the answer given is even, the nickel is in the right hand; if odd, the nickel is in the left hand.

This becomes more puzzling if you repeat it, using different multipliers and getting different answers each time. Always ask to have the coin in the right hand multiplied by an even number, the one in the left hand by an odd number.

Now, do it again, but don't ask for the answer. Point to either hand and ask that the value of the coin it holds be multiplied by 16. When the spectator says he has done this, tell him to do the same with the coin in the other hand. As soon as he says he has this answer, tell him which hand holds which coin. Your clue is that it takes him longer to multiply 5 by 16 than 10 by 16.

multiple mind reading

Several spectators mentally select cards, and the performer finds them all. The trick works itself.

From a shuffled deck, deal out five piles of five cards each. Pick up one pile, spread the cards in a fan, show them to a spectator on your left, ask him to mentally select one card and remember it. You must remember that this spectator is No. 1. Square the cards and hold the packet in your left hand.

Show a second group of five cards to a second person whom you remember as being No. 2. Place these five cards in your left hand on the first five. Repeat with three more persons. You must remember which person looked at the first packet, which saw the second, and so on — an easy matter, if you proceed from left to right, in order.

Now deal five cards in a row, then the next five on these, and so on just as you would if you were dealing five hands in a card game.

Pick up any pile, spread the cards in a fan, faces toward

the spectators, and ask if anyone sees the card he selected. Since each group now contains one card from each of the original heaps, the replies you get tell you everything you need to know. If the spectator whom you have remembered as No. 2, because he selected a card from the second heap, says that he now sees his card, you know that it is the second card from the right in the group you hold. If he selected a card from the fourth heap, his card is now fourth from the right.

Sometimes one heap will contain none of the selected cards, and another will contain two or more.

Vary the manner in which you find each card. First, spread the cards out, face up, run your fingers across them, and ask the spectator to think "Stop" when you are pointing at his card. Do the same with the next group, but with the cards face down so that you cannot see the faces. Next time, close your eyes, simply deal the cards, and when you come to the correct one toss it out face up. Finally, hold each card against the spectator's forehead, and pretend to get a vibration on the thought-of card.

These variations are red herrings which conceal the fact that you are counting, and also make your pretense of mind reading more dramatic.

x-ray eyes

An extremely mystifying two-person stunt which you and one of your children can do together. You introduce him (or her) as The Boy (or Girl) with X-ray Eyes, and he demonstrates that he can see through various solid objects.

Send him into another room. Then show several coins, one of which is chosen by a spectator and hidden under a cup. The X-ray Eye wizard returns, looks down through the cup, and not only names the coin but tells which side is up. The test is repeated and made more difficult. The coin is covered by a book, and then by several books, but his phenomenal vision penetrates these just as easily.

An extremely simple signaling system is used, but no one is likely to detect it because it changes each time the feat is repeated. On the first trial, when you cover the coin with the cup, you leave a clue as to the coin's value by the direction in which the cup handle points. If it points north (from your assistant's point of view), the coin is a penny. East indicates a nickel; south means a dime; and west, a quarter. Any other direction indicates a half dollar.

After the wizard pretends to look through the cup and names the coin, he pauses. Then, if you ask him which side is up, he says "Heads"; but if you say nothing, he says that it is tails up.

He leaves the room again and another coin is selected. You say, "*I wonder if he can see through something as thick as this.*" You cover the coin with a book, and then place the cup on the book. This time leave the cup handle pointing in the same direction as before, but place the book so that its spine faces the direction that indicates the value of the coin.

On the third trial you say, "*This time we'll make it really difficult,*" and you cover the chosen coin with more books. This time, it is the number of additional books placed on the coin which gives the clue. One book indicates a penny; two, a nickel; three, a dime; four, a quarter; five, a half dollar.

As a final demonstration which appears far more difficult than anything that has gone before, a playing card, chosen at random and seen by no one, is hidden under the stack of books. The wizard, returning to the room, again uses his X-ray vision and names it.

As you announce this test, you bring out a deck of cards and hold it in such a way that The Boy with the X-ray Eyes can, with a glance in your direction, note the bottom card. After he leaves the room, shuffle the deck without disturbing the bottom card (page 98), place the deck before a spectator, and ask him to cut it into two portions. Then pick up the lower half of the deck and place it crosswise on the top half.

Now, if you take the attention of the spectators away from the cards for a moment, they will forget exactly what was just done. Turn to the stack of books, lift them off the coin, and remove it.

Then turn back to the cards, lift the upper portion of the deck, slide out the bottom card, and put it to one side, face down. *"We'll take the card to which you cut and place it under the books without anyone having seen it."*

This is a misstatement because this card is actually the original bottom card of the deck, but if you speak matter-of-factly and keep going, no one will doubt you. Pile the books on the card, and perhaps add several more books to make it seem very difficult.

Recall The X-ray Eye Boy for the grand finale. He should pretend to have great difficulty seeing through so many books. Then he takes one book away, and, still pretending difficulty, names the card. *"That's very hard to see because it's face down and I have to look through the card, too. But it seems to be red . . . it is probably a heart . . . and it has five . . . no, six spots."*

10

MAGICAL PARTY STUNTS

the moebius strip race

A party stunt with not one but three surprise endings.

You need four strips of paper each about two inches wide and about eight feet long. Adding machine tape is perfect. Number each strip lightly with pencil near one end so that you will be able to tell them apart later. Prepare them as follows:

Strip 1. Paste the ends together, forming a circular loop, (fig. 45A, top).

Strip 2. Give one end a half twist before pasting it to the other end (fig. 45A, middle). This forms a topological structure known as a Moebius strip. You have, believe it or not, constructed a paper strip that has only *one* side and *one* edge. You can prove this (but use a short strip of paper) by drawing a pencil line down the center of the paper. Your

154

A

figure 45

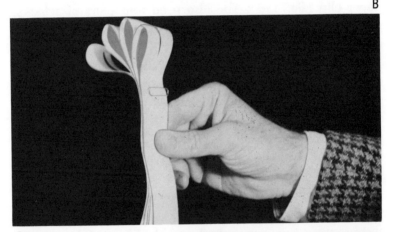

B

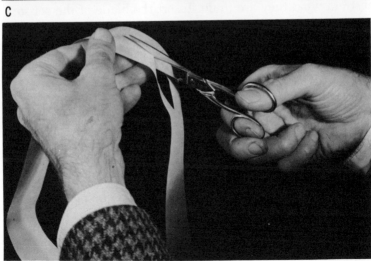

C

pencil will return to its original starting point without ever having been lifted.

Strip 3. Give one end a *full* twist before pasting it to the other end (fig. 45A, bottom).

Strip 4. Prepare this in the same way as Strip 2.

Cut an inch-long slit in each strip like the one shown in fig. 45B. In the first three strips the slit should be centered between the side edges. In the fourth strip the slit should be off-center, one-third of the distance from the right edge.

Long strips of paper are used so that the twists won't be noticed and the bands will appear to be alike. Arrange the strips in one, two, three, four order and fasten them with a paper clip (fig. 45B). You also need four pairs of scissors, preferably with blunt ends, so that no one will cut himself in the excitement.

Announce a race, with a prize for the winner. Select four children as contestants. Pick the oldest boy and the smallest girl — provided she isn't too young to use scissors — and two others.

Give Strip 1 to the little girl, Strip 4 to the big boy, and Strips 2 and 3 to the others. Also give them each a pair of scissors.

"*These loops,*" you announce, "*are race tracks. Your scissors are horses.*" Take the little girl's strip (No. 1) and demonstrate what they are to do. Insert the blade of the scissors in the slit and begin cutting down the center of the strip (fig. 45C). "*At the starting signal, everyone will begin to cut his loop into two halves — like this. Since this little girl is younger than the others, it is only fair that we give her a bit of a head start.*" Cut for about two feet down the center of her paper so that they all get the idea.

"*Everybody cut right down the center of the paper — except you.*" Turn to the boy who has Strip 4. "*You cut where your slit is, about one third of the way from the side, because I want you to make me one wide loop and one narrow one.*"

As soon as everyone is in starting position, say, *"The first person to cut his loop of paper into two separate loops will be awarded a 186-piece breakfast set! On your marks! Get set! Go!"*

Be sure to specify *two separate loops* because that is what almost no one is going to get. It's a fixed race!

This is what will happen. The little girl with Strip 1 should finish first since she had a head start. And she gets what she should — two separate loops.

But the child with Strip 2 gets a surprise. He will find that he has somehow managed to cut his strip, not into two loops, but into one loop twice as large as the original.

The child with Strip 3 does get two loops, but they are inexplicably linked together.

And the big boy with Strip 4 finishes last, because when he cuts down the side of the paper instead of down the center, he will have to cut around his original loop twice to reach his starting point. And, instead of getting one wide and one narrow loop, he gets two loops the same width, linked together — one of them twice the size of the other!

"I don't understand why three smart-looking children like you are unable to follow such simple instructions. This little girl is the only one who knows how to cut a strip of paper into two separate halves — and so she wins the 186-piece breakfast set!"

Present her with a box of corn flakes. *"If you send in the box top and ten dollars in stamps, the company will put your monogram on each piece!"*

Another way of running the race, if you can round up enough scissors, is to give strips to all the guests and let them all compete for the prize. They all get twisted loops and unexpected results except the one to whom you have given the untwisted loop. At a birthday party, of course, see that the birthday child wins.

door prize

This party trick has audience participation, drama, suspense, excitement, and is a first-rate mystery as well. The performer announces a drawing for a door prize. He shows four envelopes and states that one contains a five-dollar bill. Three children each choose an envelope and, although they all have a perfectly free choice, each selected envelope is found to contain a stick of chewing gum. The remaining envelope which nobody wanted is the one which contains the prize money.

The props required are four small envelopes (coin envelopes are perfect), six sticks of chewing gum, and a sheet of cardboard (about the size of those which laundries put in men's shirts) which you will use as a tray.

Number the envelopes serially on the face with a Magic Marker (fig. 46A). Put a stick of gum in each and seal it. Remove the wrapper from a fifth stick of gum, replace the gum with a five-dollar bill folded to gum size and rewrap it. Place this on the underside of the cardboard tray near one edge and parallel to it. The position is such that when the tray is held in the left hand the fingers cover and conceal the stick. Make a clip to hold the gum in this position by cutting a piece of cardboard about the size of a stick of gum. Glue this to the underside of the tray, one end overlapping the five-dollar stick and holding it in position (fig. 46B). Spread the four numbered envelopes on the upper surface of the tray.

Have three children come up to assist you before saying anything about a prize; otherwise you'll be mobbed. Then get your tray, holding it so that the stick of gum on its underside is hidden by the fingers of your left hand.

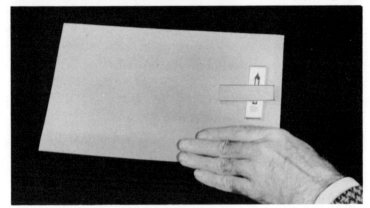

figure 46

Announce the door prize drawing, and hold up two or three of the envelopes so they can be seen. *"I have four numbered envelopes, one of which contains a five-dollar bill for the lucky winner."* Turn to the first child. *"You may take any one of these envelopes. This is a very important decision you have to make, so think it over carefully. Five dollars is a lot of money."* After he has made his choice tell him not to open his envelope until the drawing is completed.

Each of the others also selects an envelope. Then, hold up the one that remains. *"It's much too expensive to give away five dollars every time I do this so I always keep one for myself. Now, before we see who won I want to be quite sure that everyone is satisfied with his choice. Each of you may have one chance to trade envelopes with anybody else, including me."* Ask each child in turn whether he is satisfied or whether he wants to make a trade.

Because a magician is always suspect, the first child often wants to trade with you. They assume that you know which envelope contains the money, so if you look disappointed when the exchange is made, the others will want to trade with him. If you seem pleased when someone trades with you someone else will want the envelope *you* have.

Prolong this trading business, which can be very funny, by giving them each a second and absolutely final chance to make a trade. Then continue to build the suspense by having them open their envelopes, one at a time.

As this begins, place *your* envelope on the tray, sliding it under your left thumb which is directly above the concealed five-dollar gum. Then pull the tray away with your right hand and put it aside. This automatically leaves the extra stick of gum in your left hand, beneath the envelope. Turn envelope and gum up into a vertical position, and hold them in your left hand. Your thumb, at the back, holds the gum package in position. Hold the envelope fairly close to your body so that no one can see behind it.

After all the other envelopes have been opened, tear off the end of yours. Put your forefinger down into the envelope, your thumb going behind it (fig. 46C). Pull the gum at the back up into view, as though taking it from inside, and say, "That's odd! I got gum, too!"

Get rid of the envelope (and the legitimate stick of gum it still contains) by dropping it into your pocket. Slide off the outside wrapper of the gum you hold, open the inner wrapper, look surprised and pleased, and unfold the five-dollar bill.

paper puzzle

Child audiences all too often contain at least one little monster who once owned a magic set and who thinks he is an authority on the subject. No matter what you do, he makes a nuisance of himself by claiming he knows how it is done. You handle this by setting and springing a booby trap that will make him less eager to be so vocal.

Have him come up and assist you. Give him a sheet of paper and ask if he thinks he can tear it into four pieces all the same shape and size. This seems simple enough, because all he needs to do is to fold it twice and tear along the creases. When he says he can, tell him, *"It isn't as easy as it looks. If you can do it so that no piece is more than half an inch larger or smaller than the others I'll give you a quarter."*

This incentive is irresistible. Besides, even if he suspects there's a catch somewhere it's too late to back down. But he's usually cautious and the extreme amount of care with which he proceeds to accomplish this simple feat is often very funny.

When he finally gives you the four pieces, examine them carefully, measuring one against another. Then say, *"I didn't think you could do it, but I guess I lose. I'll have to pay off."*

Pause a moment so he can enjoy his triumph, then hand him one of the torn papers. *"You can have this quarter. I'll keep the other three."*

You can also have fun with this by letting several people, adults as well as children, attempt the feat at the same time. Of course, if you are outnumbered, you may have to make a quick exit at the finish.

bill catch

A feat that looks easy but proves to be next to impossible. Use a fairly new and unwrinkled dollar bill. Hold it at one end as in fig. 47. Place the thumb and forefingers of your other hand on opposite sides of the bill at the center but without touching it. Let the bill drop from your right hand and catch it with your left.

State that this is an extremely difficult feat which you have spent years practicing. No one will believe this; it looks much too easy. But they get a surprise when you let them try it. You hold the bill and your victim tries to catch it. He may hold his fingers at the bill's center as close together as

figure 47

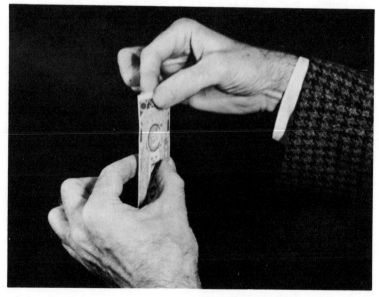

he likes, provided he is not touching it. It is easy to catch the bill when you hold it yourself because you know when it is going to fall. But when you hold it for someone else to catch and then drop it without warning, it slips between his fingers before he can close them on it.

You can pretend to give warning by counting, "*One! Two! Three! Go!*" Drop the bill a split second before you say "Go!" Or, wait until he has closed his fingers on the bill too soon, and then release it just as he opens them again. The bill escapes before his brain can reverse its order to the hand.

follow the leader

An amusing magical way to award a party prize. The performer gives a child five playing cards, takes five himself, and then performs a simple sequence of actions, turning some of the cards face up, others face down. The child follows the leader and duplicates each action exactly. At the end the performer's cards are all face down but the child has somehow managed to make a mistake: one of his is face up.

Several children are then given packets of cards. They all compete at once and all make the same mistake. On a third trial, the birthday child succeeds and wins the prize. If it is not a birthday party, then the youngest child wins, outdoing all the older ones. The losers never know what they did wrong; the winner doesn't know how he succeeded.

You need a simple gimmick. Take two cards from another deck which has the same back design and rubber cement them together face to face. Put this double-backed card on top of your deck, and place six other cards above it.

"We are," you announce, "*going to play a game of Follow the Leader. The winner will get a prize.*" Select a child to be the first contestant, and have him stand beside you facing the others.

"Before we start, you have to pass an arithmetic test. Can you count as high as five?" Deal the first five cards into his hand as he counts them aloud. *"That's perfect! But maybe you were just lucky. Think you could do it again?"*

Now count five cards for yourself into your right hand. Place each card *under* the preceding one so that their order remains the same, and so that the double-backed card is second from the top. During this count, keep the deck tipped forward so that the spectators can not see the faces of the cards. Put the remainder of the deck aside.

"Now comes the hard part. But if you can follow the leader as well as you can count, you'll probably win the prize right away. Do exactly as I do. If you don't make any mistakes you will win." Then perform the following action in slow motion, giving these instructions as you do so:

1. Turn the top card face up and put it on the bottom.
2. Put the next card on the bottom, face down.
3. Turn the next card face up and put it on the bottom.
4. Put the next card on the bottom, face down.

"You seem to be doing all right so far. Let's check." Spread your cards, showing that the first, third, and fifth are face down, and the other two face up. The contestant spreads his cards and finds that he has the same arrangement. *"You're doing fine. You've got the prize practically won. Now see if you can follow this."*

1. Turn the whole packet over.
2. Turn the top face-up card face down.
3. Turn the whole packet over again.
4. Turn the top face-down card face up.
5. Turn the whole packet over once more.

If you run through this sequence with the cards in hand, you'll see that it is easy to memorize.

Spread your cards and show that they are all face down. The contestant spreads his and finds one face up. *"That's too bad. You were doing so well, too. Well, I warned you that this wasn't easy. Would you like to try again?"*

The double-backed card in your packet is now third from the top, but must be second from the top so that you can repeat. Simply transfer the top card to the bottom as you talk. Then pick up the face-down deck, place your cards on top, and turn the deck face up.

Ask if anyone else would like to try for the prize. The response will be unanimous. If the group is a small one give everyone five cards, dealing them from the face of the deck. With a large group, pass cards out to four or five children in the first row. Then reverse the deck, take the same cards you had before for yourself, and put the deck aside.

Repeat as before. All the spectators who have cards follow your actions. At the finish your cards are again all face down; the others all find one card face up. Remember that kids love to cross up a magician, so keep an eye on them at this point to make sure that somebody doesn't try to win the prize by secretly reversing his face-up card.

Now give them one last chance. Ask the child whom you want to win the prize to come forward. If he already has some cards, take them from him for a moment as you show him where you want him to stand. Put his packet on your own, letting it overlap at the inner end. Then, when you return the cards to him, give him your packet instead.

Go through the routine again. At the end, don't bother to show your cards; they will assume you succeeded. This time everyone fails except the child who has the packet containing the double-backed card. As soon as he spreads them out (and before he can turn them over to do any investigating) take the cards from him and show the others that he has succeeded. Then give him the prize.

modern witchcraft

A trick which is made to order for children's entertainment

because of its audience participation and comedy.

Two spectators assist the magician. One chooses a card, the other tries to find it with a device which the magician says is a super-hetrodyne double-oscillating magic projector, although it looks suspiciously like an ordinary hand-powered egg beater.

You also need two faked cards which can be prepared in a few minutes beforehand. Use cards which can be easily identified at some distance, such as two Sixes of Hearts. Apply a coating of rubber cement to the face of one of these, covering an area about a half-inch wide along the lower edge of the card. Take any other card and put rubber cement on its back in the same way. Let the cement dry for a moment, then cover the face of the Six of Hearts with the second card, align them carefully, and press the cemented surfaces together. This forms a double card which is joined at one end only (fig. 48A).

Curl a three-inch length of Scotch tape back on itself to form a ring with the sticky surface outside. Attach this to the back of the other Six of Hearts across one end, and flatten it out (fig. 48B). Place the double card, face down, on a face-down packet of nine or ten indifferent cards, and put the Scotch-taped card on top. The end of the card bearing the tape should be at the opposite end of the packet from the joined ends of the double card.

These cards and an egg beater are on your table covered with a handkerchief so that they are not seen until you are ready to start the trick. Begin by asking two spectators, preferably a boy and a girl, to assist you. Ask the girl to stand on your left, the boy on your right. Then get the egg beater and tell the girl, "*You'll never guess what this is.*"

When she replies that it is an egg beater, act surprised. "*An egg beater? Gosh, I never thought of that! Perhaps you could beat eggs with it. But that's not what it is. This is a super-hetrodyne double-oscillating magic projector. I bor-*

figure 48

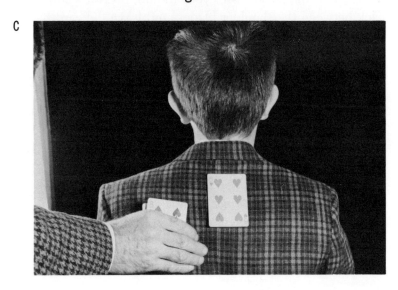

rowed it from a friend of mine who is a witch. This thing at the end is called a handle, and you hold it in your left hand. That's your left hand over there. This little wheel on the side of the projector is an oscillating crank which you have to turn by hand. My friend, the witch, also has a new power model but the carburetor isn't working and it's being repaired."

Give the egg beater to the girl and explain that the device is held horizontally and aimed like a gun. *"When you turn the crank, magic rays come out at the revolving end. But don't turn it until I tell you to because it might backfire and that's dangerous. And whatever you do, don't drop it! I have to return it to the witch in good condition before midnight. If I don't, she'll turn us both into pumpkins. I doubt if your mother would like that."*

Get the packet of cards and hold them face down in your right hand, your thumb lying across and hiding the Scotch tape.

Take the boy by the arm and lead him to the right, six feet or so away from the girl. *"You stand here, and face the audience."* Turn him into this position and, at the same time, put your right hand which holds the cards behind him. Push the top card off the packet with your thumb, press it against his back between the shoulder blades, and leave the card hanging there (fig. 48**C**).

Then spread the other cards a bit and give the boy and the audience a brief look at their faces — long enough so that the cards are seen to be different. *"We'll also use these cards."*

Square the packet, turn it face down, and shuffle the cards overhand. Pull the double card off first, then shuffle the others onto it. Shuffle again, letting the double card fall last so that it is returned to the top.

Tell the boy, *"I want you to remember one of these cards. It doesn't matter which one. This will do."* As you say this, lift up the outer (uncemented) edge of the top card and let him see the Six of Hearts. You may want to mark this end of the card with a small pencil dot in the white margin of the back so that you can always tell which is the uncemented edge.

Give the cards another quick shuffle, and lose the double card among the others. Hold the packet of cards out on a line with the egg beater and halfway between the boy and the girl. Tell the girl, *"Please aim the projector at the cards and turn the crank when I give the signal. The magic rays will make the card he's thinking of fly out and sail across the room."* Turn to the boy. *"And you see if you can catch it."*

Look at the girl, then step over and change the aim of the projector slightly. *"Don't point that at me! It's dangerous! Point it at him."*

Start the countdown. *"Ready! Get set! . . ."* Stop, look at the boy and ask, *"Are you nervous?"* No matter what he replies, tell him, *"You should be. This is the first time I've used this machine. Anything could happen!"*

Repeat the count, *"Ready! Get set! Go!"* When the girl begins cranking, vibrate the hand holding the cards as though it were receiving an electric shock. Stop the girl, then look at the boy. *"You didn't catch the card? I'm sure I felt it go."* Go to him, ask, *"Is it still there?"* Count the cards one at a time into your left hand so that he can see them all. He has to admit that the card is not there.

"Maybe it flew into one of your pockets." He looks but doesn't find it. *"Turn around once; it must be here somewhere."* When he turns around, the spectators see it on his back. Then you see it. *"Gosh! It went right through him!"*

Remove the card and show it to him. *"I'm very sorry. I hope it didn't hurt much."* Ask him to take a bow. Congratulate the girl on her aim and have her take a bow, too.

arithmetic race

Try this on the child who is learning to add. It makes a

game out of his homework. Ask him to write down any number between one and ten. You add to this any number which is ten or less. Then he does the same, and you each continue to add numbers alternately until the total reaches one hundred. The player who hits that number wins the game.

You can always win, simply by hitting one of the following key numbers: 12, 23, 34, 45, 56, 67, 78, 89. These are easily remembered because in each instance, the second digit is one more than the first. Having brought the total to any one of the key numbers you can hit all the others merely by noting the number your opponent adds and adding enough more to make eleven. Once you reach eighty-nine your opponent has lost because no matter what number he adds you can bring it to one hundred.

After you have won a few games, explain the system to the child so he can try it on his friends. This gives all of them some adding practice.

coin quiz

Place three coins in a row an inch or two apart. Adjust them carefully as though it were very important to get the space between them just right. Offer a prize to the first child who can tell, without measuring, which two coins are farthest apart. Tell them to raise their hands as soon as they have the answer. Some hands never go up, and this gets a laugh because the answer is so absurdly easy. It's the two coins at the ends of the row, of course.

coin problem

Place two coins, A and B, side by side and touching. The problem is to move a third coin in between the first two, but coin A must not be touched in any way and coin B must not be moved. Most people give up on this one.

Solution: Put a finger on B so that it cannot move, then hit it sharply on the edge directly opposite coin A by sliding the third coin against it. A, which hasn't been touched will be knocked away from B which hasn't been moved, leaving space to insert the third coin.

knot puzzler

Have someone hold a length of string, rope, or a scarf by opposite ends. Ask him to tie a knot in it *without letting go of either end*. When he objects that this is impossible, reach out quickly, grasp the ends as shown in fig. 49, and pull them in opposite directions. A knot forms instantly. *"Nothing hard about that,"* you say. *"It's easy."*

The spectator, having seen everything, usually says that he can also do it if you hold the ends. He seldom suceeds because he finds that he can't remember just how you crossed your arms. *"I'll do it again,"* you say. *"Keep one eye on my right hand, one eye on my left hand, and one eye on the rope."*

You can sometimes repeat the tie several times before anyone duplicates it. Give the first person to succeed a prize,

figure 49

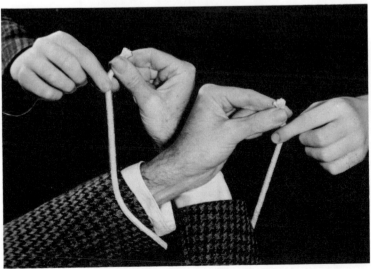

then fifteen minutes later ask him to do it again. The chances are that he has already forgotten how.

bottle lift

Offer a prize to the first person who can lift a pop bottle with a soda straw. You seldom have to pay off on this one.

Solution: Bend the straw back on itself three or four inches from one end. Push the double end down into the bottle and lift (fig. 50).

the imprisoned coin

Invert a drinking glass over a coin. Put another upside-

figure 50

figure 51

down glass near it and wedge a kitchen match between the glasses (fig. 51). Note that the head of the match is placed against the empty glass. The problem is to remove the coin without letting the match fall and without touching the match.

Solution: Light the head of the match with a second match and blow out the flame as soon as the head burns. The match will now adhere to the empty glass, allowing the other glass to be lifted and the coin removed. Warning: *Don't* use plastic glasses.

checker stack

Make a stack of half a dozen checkers and offer a prize to the first person who can remove the bottom checker, using only a table knife. None of the other checkers may be touched or dislodged.

Solution: A quick blow on the side of the bottom checker with the knife blade will knock it out. Be sure to follow through so that the knife also passes beneath the stacked checkers.

match lift

Anyone who figures this out for himself deserves whatever prize you offer. It is a neat problem in engineering. How do you lift seven matches with only one match?

Solution: See fig. 52.

the one-move mystery

Place six glasses or paper cups in a row and fill the three on the left with whatever drink you are serving. The problem is to rearrange things so that the glasses are alternately full and empty, but only one glass may be touched or moved.

Solution: Lift the second glass from the left and pour its contents into the second glass from the right.

marksmanship

Announce a marksmanship contest and give the first contestant half a dozen playing cards. Place a hat, brim up, at his feet and ask him to drop the cards, one at a time, from shoulder height into the hat. Offer a party prize for high score and a more valuable prize, perhaps a money prize, for a perfect score.

Everyone will be eager to try; it looks easy. But no one, unless they've seen it before, is likely to have much success. The usual score is: none. When the cards are held and dropped edge down, which seems to be the obvious way to

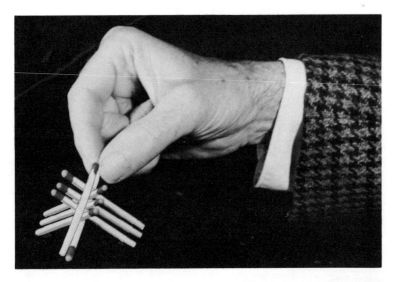

figure 52

do it, they fall straight for about a foot, then begin turning somersaults and go to one side.

Pay off for high score if anyone accidentally gets one or two into the hat. Then show that it is not only possible but easy to get a perfect score — when you know how. When the cards are held horizontally and dropped flat, they float down into the hat like homing pigeons.